The Reverend Canon Quine has a psychic gift: when those on 'the other side' choose to offer comfort and advice to those left behind, he has been able to pass on their messages. He is a spiritual healer, and has enjoyed some very positive successes.

Without sensationalism, he discusses how he receives these messages through 'guides', and on the way introduces us to the multiplicity of interesting characters that he has met over the years – both from this world and the next one. But this is not just the story of one man's physic experiences. Canon Quine has explored the phenomenon extensively, asking questions both of himself and of his fellow psychics – some of whom appear to have even more extraordinary gifts than the author himself. The result is *Living Proof*, a glimpse of a world beyond and a challenge to the sceptics who deny the possibility of life after physical death.

The Reverend Canon Quine went to university in Durham and has an honours degree in theology, a Durham M. A. and is a Ph. D of Nottingham University. He became a canon of Leicester Cathedral in 1967 and for 32 years was Vicar of Belgrave. The author has contributed to many television and radio programmes and has written often for *The Leicester Mercury*. A keen sportsman, Canon Quine is President of his local bowls club and a member of the Leicester Tigers Rugby Club.

LIVING PROOF

Is There Life After Death?

Ken Quine

The Book Guild Ltd
Sussex, England

The Book Guild Ltd.
25 High Street,
Lewes, Sussex

First published 1996
© Ken Quine, 1996
Set in Times
Typesetting by Raven Typesetters, Chester

Printed in Great Britain by
Athenaeum Press Ltd
Gateshead.

A catalogue record for this book is
available from the British Library

ISBN 1 85776 064 6

Contents

PREFACE

I have been constantly urged by people to set down many of the things which they have found to be a source of help and encouragement.

Following a series of articles in the local newspaper some time ago I am asked wherever I go 'When are you going to write that book?' Time has been in short supply but I feel I must now try to reach a wider circle of people who might be encouraged by the record of my own personal experiences with some reference to those friends who share a gift.

Lest there be any misunderstanding

I draw a distinction between 'life' and 'continuing to live'. In my ministry, sadly, I have met many people who continue to live but their quality of life is drastically poor. Sometimes this is due to deprivation or illness or to the actions of other people; sometimes it is the fault of the person. One of the reasons for this book is to show that there is continuation of life in the world beyond this life. There is however far more to the teaching of Jesus than that.

Vibrant spiritual life in harmony with the will of God who is absolute goodness, love and justice and who holds all eternal power, is not the same as just continuing to live. Jesus taught that God wants *real life* for every living soul, the realisation of which can begin here and now, reaching forward to a wonderful reality in, to give it His term, 'The Kingdom of Heaven'. This is God's plan for us. This is what we aim for by His Grace. Just to continue to live on the first plane of existence after life in this world, is not the full reality of what Jesus wants for you and for me. I wish to make this very clear at the outset. God does not just want us to continue to exist – full stop. He is offering us something beyond our comprehension almost – a quality of life to which we are to progress by His forgiveness, power and love and by joining our own free will which he has given to us, with the Divine Will. By so doing there is created a wonderful and harmonious relationship between God and us, as was shown to us in the person of Jesus Christ. This is our greatest good although we act so seldom as if we realise it.

No misunderstanding then! I want to suggest to you from my experiences that there is continuation of life after life in this world, but there is far more to it than mere existence.

1

The Question Asked

I am aware that this book will cause a flutter in the dovecotes. Canons of the church who write about their psychic experiences are few and far between.

I am writing for ordinary people. There is greater interest in the paranormal than at any time in my life and, although we are well behind in these matters compared with the USA; a chair has been established at Lancaster University to investigate parapsychology. This book is not an attempt to investigate along those lines or to emulate the kind of writing in that excellent little publication, edited by the Former Archdeacon of Durham entitled *The Christian Parapsychologist* (CFPSS)[1]. I am simply setting down my experiences. I am not, for instance, going to tackle the relationship between the conscious and subconscious mind and their connection with 'cosmic wholeness' of which we are all a part. I am simply going to offer my experiences as an answer to a simple question; can we, in certain circumstances be in touch with those in the continuation of life, the next world, call it what you will, so that we are sure of that contact beyond any shadow of doubt? My contention is that from time to time those who have entered that world have made their presence known and continue to do so.

I have taken a long time before setting down these experiences because I am reluctant to encourage people to think that psychic experience obviates the need for true religion. The truth is that the psychic faculty is not in itself good or bad. For instance oratory is neither good or bad. It can be used either as in the past by a certain

---

[1] There are many books like Gittelson's *Intangible Evidence* (Simon and Schuster) which attempt to summarise all kinds of psychic activities

Bishop of the Church who was given the name 'Golden Mouthed', or by Hitler's Propaganda Minister who poisoned the minds of hundreds of thousands of decent young people. Psychic ability can be dedicated and used for good. It can be used wrongly but the idea that anything psychic is always wrong is nonsense.

I have no doubt that readers wish to get on with reading about the experiences I have mentioned but a little background is necessary first. There is scepticism among journalists investigating psychic matters. Who can blame them? There is no area which is so open to fraud and manipulation, to imagination and self-deception. The journalist is sent out to investigate the activity of some famous medium and his editor sees excellent copy in those situations which turn out to be exaggerated or seem to be untrue. More space is given to those situations than to those which often seem genuine. Sometimes statements in books by mediums are found to be inaccurate. This may be due to lapse of memory where no notes are kept and and sometimes they are due to the fact that mediums employ ghost writers who tend to 'write up' events and themselves have no means of proving whether the medium is remembering correctly, nor perhaps have they the time or motivation to investigate every claim as a journalist might. I am afraid that so often the use of the psychic gift on a distinctive commercial basis goes wrong. It is not always the case of course but often the hiring of large halls and the charging of hefty sums for admission overshadow what is trying to be proved. Some mediums who have a gift are tempted on to an ego trip. They like the publicity but the press is soon on to the mistakes that are made.

We must be fair. Have you ever thought that only God is right all the time? Have you ever met a human being who has never made a mistake? The strange thing is that we expect mediums to be right all the time. This is silly. It is just not going to happen. We have the right to expect them to be honest and to expose them if they are not. The questions however that we must consider are; are they right sometimes? and are they right so often that what they say demands careful consideration? I find people ranging from Bishops to laymen dismiss the core of what mediumship is saying without any knowledge on their part and after no investigation, yet they would claim to be part of this scientific age. It is not a matter of life and death to me to be proved right as long as the reader will do me the courtesy of thinking hard about what I write.

Many orthodox church people are going to be annoyed with me because they will think that I am leading people to place their trust other than in God in Jesus Christ. In the church where I was vicar, Jesus Christ was preached with love and conviction and everything revolved around that. I need hardly say that the psychic played no part in our worship and spiritual life. I believe the psychic simply to be the tool of the spiritual. It has its uses. God is the Father of all people even if they are all at different spiritual levels of understanding. Sometimes the psychic can help a seeker. Sometimes it cannot because that seeker needs a quite different experience.Those who have not 'seen', who exercise deep faith without any psychic experience must be content often to hear of others who have needed a spur to faith not so afforded to themselves.

Books by mediums usually begin with a description of their childhood experiences. In fact, at one stage, I met so many mediumistic people who had seen clairvoyantly (seeing on the screen of the mind but not through the physical eye) and heard clairaudiently (hearing in the mind but not with the agency of the physical ear), since childhood that I had formed the opinion that all true mediums had always 'seen' and 'heard'. This is however, not the case and I have met a number of people who have developed this faculty as late as middle age and some beyond that.

I had very few childhood experiences. As I grew up one or two things happened which I felt were strange, but these things can be parallelled many times over in the lives of thousands of ordinary people. For instance, once, in a flash, I saw the bedroom of my mother and father. In the bed was one of my parents who I instinctively knew was desperately, fatally ill. In a few months my father had taken ill and passed onwards. On the whole such experiences were few.

My mother was a very spiritual person, almost a mystic. She had a truly remarkable mind, as notable for intelligence as for its complete openness. She condemned nothing until she had listened or read, and considered. I hope I have inherited that. However I was not a psychic prodigy. On the whole I am unhappy to hear of children who are being encouraged to exercise their psychic gift too early. I always advise parents to leave such children to enjoy their childhood and grow up naturally, and to find their faith in the teaching of the local Christian church and their worship of God uncomplicated by other considerations until they are mature enough to see their true place in the scheme of things.

I suppose my view of mediumistic affairs as a teenager was rather like that of most of my fellows. At school, in house meetings, we would often invent a sketch in which some dressed-up as old ladies, looking very weird, chanting, 'Is there anybody there?' From off stage would come a sepulchral voice groaning 'Nooooo'. This was always good for a laugh. Mediums were portrayed just as they are now in films and plays and on television as very strange people. Writers and actors have a field day with such parts. When copy is short I often think journalists find a medium to kick. Sometimes this is the fault of mediums themselves, but the finest medium I have ever known was as ordinary and pleasant a family woman as you could ever wish to meet. Her feet were planted firmly on the ground. She knew the degree of opposition to her gift and she knew the answers.

About twenty years ago I realised that many of my clergy brothers, good chaps and well meaning at heart decried everything psychic as evil but in fact they knew nothing whatsoever about psychic things. Sometimes they had encountered fraud or deception or simply imagination posing as some message from the continuation of life. Sometimes they had found that the simple faith of a person had been pushed aside and that person had begun a continuous, puerile and often damaging quest for message after message from people on the other side of life, which began to replace true worship of God and faith and trust in Him. In the Anglican church we had experts on the Roman Catholic Church, experts on Methodism and on the Eastern Orthodox Church, experts on Pastoral Psychology and the Liturgy and so I asked myself, why not on psychic matters? I decided that the only way to find out the truth was to get into the thing at grass roots and to find out from first-hand experience, not to sit back and criticise from outside. Some of my brother clergy were very critical. They

4

felt close contact was harmful. However I realised that they could not have it both ways. If you were, as they all agreed, armed with the power of the Living God, what had you to fear? I must say here, that on the whole, I have found my clergy friends very good about my journey into the psychic waters. I think they felt I was not a fool and, being known to be of a very critical mind, not likely to believe in nonsense. I am known not to be credulous in any respect. At no stage was I going to swallow nonsense from mediums. Nor did I! On the other hand I have never been unwilling to admit that I am wrong where I genuinely thought I was.

It then seemed that the way opened up. By chance I met Nella Taylor a Derbyshire woman and a Police Sergeant's widow. I was quite astonished at her knowledge of my past life and of things that even my wife and family and friends were ignorant. These things she could not possibly have researched. There was no information available to her even had she the time and ability to research it. No documentary evidence existed and often the only persons who could have verified the situations were dead. She explained to me that these things were given to her to pass on to me from someone on the other side of life, as a proof of the fact that that person was there. I went to meetings to see her exercise her gift which she used almost exclusively to prove to others that there was continuation of life after life in this world. Naturally after that I listened with an open mind to others with a similar gift and spent many hours over several years visiting, attending, listening, questioning, and meeting people with a degree of clairvoyance or clairaudience. I attended circles and groups and services with great patience. Through Mrs Taylor I met some of those who would be regarded as very advanced in this ability. I experienced remarkable physical phenomena, probably the area most open to fraud and deception and least liked by Nella Taylor. I tried to find other explanations for what I was experiencing other than those advanced to me. I had to settle right at the beginning for the fact that, as I have explained, the psychic is neither good nor bad and not the prerogative of Christian people or even God-fearing people. Before some raise their hands in horror let me remind them that neither is music, nor art, nor many other gifts. I think that I would have abandoned my task had I not been

5

impressed however with the spirituality and Christian belief of so many whom I met with this ability. Mrs Taylor herself was a convinced Christian and was the first to warn me that many who did not honour Our Lord or who did not believe in God in a personal sense, nevertheless had a fair degree of psychic ability. Many men of talent have been atheists. I was aware however, of the way Nella and those like her used their gift to guide people to seek and find and trust the great force we call God and to have faith in Him. 'You must trust Him,' I heard her say so often 'even where you cannot trace.' To many I met the evidence afforded through the psychic deepened their trust and faith in God. It was naturally among these people that I made friends. I saw very clearly the great dangers of associating with those on the other side of life who were not the servants of the Living God by their own choice, a choice they had made when on this earth and which they continued to make on the first plane of spirit[1] existence. By God's love they had continuation of life but I was not prepared to allow their influence in my life. I have to say therefore, that there are dangers in indiscriminate use of psychic ability. A child should not play with electricity. It must be taught how to control it. Too many engage in psychic activity without the spiritual base from which to move out. I would advise people strictly against using ouija boards or any devices which can be manipulated by people on the other side of life, or of thinking because they have one or two psychic experiences they will be or could be competently mediumistic. The number of 'one off' psychic experiences are numbered in hundreds of thousands. Too many people are told by those who think that they are 'teachers' in these matters that they can develop an occasional psychic experience and become mediums. When this doesn't happen, the budding medium can go through great disillusionment and even be harmed psychologically. Some will object that this alone is good reason for not having anything to do with psychic matters, I do not agree. I set out

---

[1] spirit is the word which we give to the substance of the next world and which is indestructible and eternal by God's decree. It is the parallel of matter in our present universe. I never call those who have moved into the next world 'spirits' – they are people, and always will be!

with an open mind and I came to a conclusion. More than that, despite the pitfalls, I found continuation of life after life on this earth proved by my experiences. I warn against the dangers but I hold out hope through what I have found as well as the faith which – as a minister – I constantly preach.

If I am asked whether or not psychic experience will destroy one's faith in God. I reply that it hasn't destroyed mine, in fact it has strengthened it. If I am asked whether it is not true, that in the various meetings and services up and down the country where the psychic is incorporated, the so-called philosophy is often humanistic and not worth the name, I reply that this is so. If I am asked if the messages given, purporting to come from the other side of life are sometimes trivial, I can assure you that they often are. If I am asked whether it is not true that people accept messages as true when it is quite clear they have practically fed the message to the medium, I can tell you that this is happening all the time. If I am asked if I would want all this in a church service I would reply, 'No thank you, for worship should be of God.' If the psychic has any use it should, in my view, be used on the perimeter of true worship, individually. In this I know I disagree with some of my medium friends. I remember one dear soul with a great mediumistic gift, who used to go to the Salvation Army for 'some real worship', as she put it. You might ask why did she not go there all the time? It was because she wanted to use her psychic gift to help people and there was no Orthodox Christian Church (for she was a convinced Christian) in which she could use her gift. Remember we have only recently welcomed spiritual healing in the Anglican Church. We are asking if the evidence produced by the psychic is worth considering and I hope to answer this from my own experiences with the word 'Yes'.

Now of course the commonest objection to the use of the psychic for any reason comes from those who say that it is forbidden in Scripture. I will forebear to expand the argument that it would be a very extraordinary person who lived their life in every detail according to the injunctions of Scripture which was written so long ago. It gives me great amusement at times to listen to people who engage in what I term 'bibliolotry'. I say this however as one who has a great reverence for the Bible and for the truth enshrined in it. The Bible however, records all kinds of things, ancient customs, some history – some correct – some incorrect, descriptions of worship and belief, sociology, geographical notes – some correct – some incorrect, and the record of a people's religious life in which they were led by very remarkable Men of God. The religious leaders of whom we are speaking had no small task in keeping together the religious life of the community in the face of idolotry and heathenism. Anything which seemed to take people from one clear pathway to God was to be deplored and opposed. However as I have explained the psychic gift is neither good nor bad and throughout history it has been an ability possessed by many kinds of people. The religious leaders of Israel did not want people running to heathen psychics for help. It seemed quite correct to them therefore, to declare that all such psychics were to be avoided. I cannot see that if it is true that in ancient times there were those who used the psychic gift wrongly, it means that today we must avoid using the psychic gift in the right way. Again the priestly leaders of Israel, after the demise of the great prophets wished to have a firm grip over the religious life of the people and worked over the religious literature to this end. The problem with mystics and psychics is that they are notoriously independent and in olden times were a thorn in the side of the priestly hierarchy. The way to oppose them was to give out that their gift was not from God and was to be deplored. It is very interesting however, to see how the religious leaders of Israel left behind in the religious literature clear examples of the use of psychic by their own great religious leaders.

I can remember a young man coming to me and saying, 'Vicar I have come to you because my vicar says that use of the psychic is evil – is it?' He went on to tell me that his vicar had said that the Bible was absolutely against it and, as he had some psychic ability, he was very disturbed. He had questioned a number of clergy and they had all told him to come and see me. He said that his vicar had quoted to him in scathing language the case of King Saul consulting the so-called 'Witch of Endor'. I am afraid that in ancient times anyone wanting to be very nasty to a lady with a psychic gift dubbed her a witch. A few hundred years ago hundreds and hundreds of poor souls who were just a bit 'fey' as they say in the north were burned as witches throughout Europe. The story is that King Saul wished to speak with the Prophet Samuel who had died. He went to this mediumistic lady at Endor and ordered her to 'Call up Samuel'. She duly obliged. I had to tell this young man that whether it was in the Bible or not it was not correct, because no medium can call up anyone. If our loved ones and friends come to us from the other side of life, it is because they wish to do so and they exercise the free will they have there as they had it here. They certainly cannot be *summoned*. Frankly if anyone told me a story like that today I would call it an Old Wives' Tale. However I told the young man that the best thing that he could do was to go back to his vicar and ask him if the great prophet Samuel was a medium. He would certainly say 'No' because he taught that all mediums were of the devil. I told him to ask the vicar to read again 1 Samuel; 9, in which Saul the son of Kish is sent to look for his father's herd of asses which have strayed. He is unsuccessful but his servant tells him about a Man of God who is worth consulting on the matter. They do not seem to have a suitable fee but the servant produces the fourth part of a shekel and they find Samuel. Samuel quickly deals with the matter of the lost asses and tells Saul that they have in fact been found. How did he know? He obviously used his psychic gift which was well known. Samuel had of course far more important things to show to Saul and he anointed him as the future King of Israel.

Indeed, Jesus himself was clearly mediumistic. Philip comes to Nathanael and tells him that they have found Him of whom Moses and the prophets wrote (St John; 1). Nathanael is sceptical that such a person could come from Nazareth. Philip brings him to Jesus who says to him, 'Behold an honest Jew.' Nathanael says, 'You don't know me.' Jesus says, 'Before you came here when you were under the fig tree I saw you.' The implication is clear, that fig tree was well out of sight. Nathanael knows Jesus could not have seen him with ordinary physical vision. He is impressed. Jesus is amused and tells him that such power is nothing and that he will see greater things than that. Mediums are doing such things every day of the week. On another occasion Jesus meets a woman at a well and what takes place is unusual for several reasons. First it would have been unusual for a well-known Rabbi to talk to that particular woman who was a stranger and then because he tells her about her life and her past in such a way as to quite astonish her and she goes into the village and pays testimony to his gift.

I can assure you that one does not have to be God to do such a thing, although of course only God could give the spiritual Grace Jesus urged her to seek in Him.

It is not the purpose of this book to sift through the Bible and discuss the evidence for what we now term psychic experiences. I am merely saying that it is there. For instance, Moses and Elijah appeared to Jesus who was accompanied by Peter, James and John, (St Mark; 9). It is not the purpose of this book either, to discourse on angels. The Bible often refers to the appearance of angels. Leaving aside the possibility of another order of created beings other than human beings I suggest that often these appearances are simply servants of God from the other side of life who make themselves known in His service. A very good explanation of why they 'appear' as men.

2

Longing for Survival

The greatest hope in the human breast is to survive what is very often a difficult, and sometimes a right down unhappy, life. 90 per cent of those with jobs would rather be doing something else and the sad number of those without jobs find the experience of surviving a difficult task. This all affects their families. But the drive to survive goes deeper than that. I believe that it is a natural, God-given instinct. The purpose of this book is to record my own experiences, not to make a study of primitive beliefs but any study of the latter will point to this longing for survival not only here but hereafter.

Perhaps I should say at the outset that any person who fancies a witch hunt is wasting their time perusing these pages. There have always been those in history who delight in discovering heresy where there is no heresy. I am an orthodox Christian with an honours degree in theology. I believe God came in Jesus Christ and through Him, that is through 'Perfect, Divine Love' which is the essence of His being we have God's forgiveness and His gift of Eternal Life. I am aware that certain psychics claim to have been told that Jesus was a great master like other great masters – each appearing at an appointed time in history. They teach that there are great masters alive today, although sometimes the evidence is far from convincing. I am sure that the biblical claim that God never leaves himself without a witness is true. I am sure that great masters of the spiritual life have 'appeared' by God's grace at various times in various nations and for various purposes. I do not however put them on a level with Jesus. It is through the love of God, uniquely expressed through Him, that we have forgiveness for our opposition to God's laws, and inherit God's gift to us of Eternal Life. We may fondly think that there is some other pathway rather than through Him. I do not believe that there is – however much spiritual truth can be obtained from non-Christian sources and I do not deny the importance of such truth. It is for this reason that I am wary of psychics who are atheists. There are many humanists also who have psychic ability but who have little or no interest in Jesus and some, in fact, have scant respect for God Himself. The reason for that is sometimes easy to understand. Such psychics have been put off in their earlier life by an unfortunate experience in the Church, or, often they are incensed by some aspect of sinful human nature in history enacted by people who claimed to be doing what they did in the name of the Church and of God. Instead of seeing the truth and being firm in condemnation; instead of sifting the wheat from the chaff; humanistic psychics often throw out the baby with the bath water. Others, although possessing great psychic ability, which I keep stressing is neither good nor bad and can be used in the service of good or evil, have made a link with some powerful personality on the other side of life who carries on, on the plane where he or she now exists, the self interest and opposition to the Divine Lord of All Life, which characterised their own life on earth. Whilst such psychics get psychic results of a kind they will not break away from such influences. Their ability psychically will influence many but nobody will make spiritual progress through them. That is the gauge by which their work must be measured. I am wary of any whose source of information however factually true on a low level, do not have regard for the source of all truth and power – Almighty God. Such people may well tell you about your past and sometimes predict accurately things to happen, but they will not improve spiritual knowledge and indeed will stunt spiritual growth by their teaching. Their work is strictly limited in value and must be tested and watched. They are a constant headache to groups who are willing to use the psychic to advance spiritual knowledge and regard it as the handmaid of spiritual growth and advancement.

If one could believe that by the physical body ceasing to function, one could stand on the other side of life, suddenly progressed spiritually, morally, mentally and so on, one could easily believe in fairies at the bottom of the garden. How could one expect, by the death of the physical body, to be suddenly transformed in all the essential depth of our being? In a sense I suppose, the doctrine of Purgatory wrestled with this; providing a place where sin can be expurgated and such spiritual progress made as will enable us to function in the wonderful atmosphere of the destiny God has provided. It is a short step from that to what I certainly believe, which is that we have much to learn after physical death and need to adjust by our own free will to the condition necessary in which we can live in that sphere where God's Will is continually done and sin (opposition to his Divine Goodness) is excluded. My emphasis is therefore not on something forced upon us – arranged for us – but something we must do by our own volition and that exercise of the free will is vital. I believe we rise in the continuation of life from one sphere of progress to another until we attain a state where we can enjoy what God has prepared to the full. Now I am aware that when I write this the reader will grow restless, especially if he or she has been brought up to believe in the essentiality of the 'free gift' aspect of Eternal Life. Evangelicals believe that it is by God's Love *alone* that we are forgiven and by that forgiveness do we have Eternal Life. I believe that also. Without that, there is nothing. God in His love may forgive me my sins but I don't believe that he removes from me my responsibility to put right what I have done wrong and I believe I have much to do to compensate by my own free will before I could fit into the final destiny he has prepared for me. I am not a puppet. I must surrender self willingly to His Great Love – He will not make me. To suggest therefore, despite the essentiality of God's forgiveness and the grace of the gift of Eternal Life, that I have no part to play in what he has planned is foolishness. It takes from the logic of the Divine Action. When I begin to find the kingdom within myself and let it function in my daily life I begin to progress towards the kingdom where God's Will is the norm – my ultimate destiny. I do not find this incompatible with Christian belief. It makes no sense to believe that, by chanting a religious formula or by being released from the physical body, I am therefore fit to live in the nearer presence of God. It is a steady process and to believe this does not detract for one second from the embracing nature of

God's salvation. After all if what I am saying is not true why on earth does not God just give us all 'the treatment' now and stop these terrible things men do to men. The greatness of His Love provides the destiny of us all in embryo but we must all make our own progress within the orbit of the Divine Love.

Leaving aside a long discussion on the truth or untruth of reincarnation; that is, as to whether some people come back on earth to complete or to work out experiences which they were prevented from experiencing or completing before physical death – a quite fascinating study and not so silly a notion as some would believe – I can sense the objection of some readers to what I am saying. They point to the vast numbers of people who have in turn peopled this earth. I have often been told that it would take a very large world to contain all such people, as if this was quite impossible. I do not believe that is so. I believe that the spheres on the other side of life are vast beyond comprehension. Beside them this universe and all known universes are a pinhead. I believe the creation of God is huge and that we should get some inkling of this from our scientific friends who astound us with the tremendous figures of space measurement which they use when lecturing on space. They teach us that there are millions of universes like our own. I believe that what lies beyond on the other side of physical and material creation is even vaster. God cannot be contained nor His creative activity limited in any respect except by His own Divine Wisdom.

I believe therefore that on the other side of life there is ample 'room' for all who go forward there. It does not matter whether one has been a Bishop, a great politician or some well-known public figure, or whether one has been what we so glibly call an 'ordinary person' (are there any *ordinary* people?) in that immediate sphere after this life, as after reaching that sphere, we shall be known not by any earthly title or accomplishment, but by our 'light'. 'Let your light so shine before men,' said Jesus that men may see what kind of person you are. In the continuation of life we shall be seen to be what we are by our light. Those who have made spiritual progress find doors open to them in the corridors of light which lead them to further spheres of progress in due course. Those who have chosen, by their own free will (not those who are

14

victims of ignorance for whom provision is made) to waste their time on earth with the purely material, find that they have much to do all over again. They have had equal chance with others who have responded to God's goodness and His wish for them which is their greatest good. They have nobody to blame but themselves for turning their backs on this. If they haven't had the opportunities to hear about God's Love and his plan for them, I believe they are still given that chance. It doesn't follow that, because they are on the plane immediately beyond the earth plane, that they will respond quickly or willingly – they still have free will!

If this is true and I believe that it is, then when we consider this first sphere of life on the other side of the earth life, sometimes called the Astral plane, or the Lower Astral Plane, – various names are given to it and argued about – we shall find like attracted to like. Those who choose deliberately to oppose the goodness of God, find their affinity with others like themselves by their own choice. Others, whilst by no means perfect have the longing to progress further and do better and have learned the lessons which we should all learn on this earth and gravitate to those who are like minded. I am not saying of course that it is all black or white, one or the other. I am saying that the desire to progress forward spiritually is a far more dominating factor there than it appears to be here, clogged down by the material.

This all means that we, who are on the earth plane of existence must show great care in communicating with those on the immediate sphere beyond this life. We have to be sure of the integrity of the person communicating with us; to accept uncritically any communication from the other side of life is foolish. Whilst all proved communications are interesting from a technical point of view so to speak, I for one would be very wary of any communication through an avowed exponent of godlessness in any form. The psychic gift therefore is not a plaything as we shall discover later on in this book. It needs developing carefully under expert guidance and under those who value the spiritual more than the psychic. Unhappily there is a dearth of very able, spiritually minded, Christian teaching mediums.

I realise that some people will already be questioning statements I have made in the preceding pages which refer to

15

conditions in the continuation of life. They will be asking them-selves, 'How does he know?' The simple outline I have given comes from the many things said by those on the other side of life and to me they are logical and intelligent. As to whether such people are able to say these things the reader will have to judge from the evidence which follows.

3

Beginnings

You will never hear me talk about or write about 'spirits'. I find such a word is bound to confuse people. It suggests beings who are rather less than complete in some way. Those on the other side of life are in every way not only as integrated and completely whole persons as any of us here on earth but they often show that they are not clogged down with the material aspects of this world. I never use the word 'ghost'. I never refer to a person on the other side of life as 'it'. We must learn to treat them always as beings like ourselves. After all we have known many of them personally in our own lives and loved them dearly.

I am quite sure that the best way to set people thinking is simply to dip into the hundreds of experiences I have had in my ministry which point to the continuation of life and offer them for consideration. Some will appeal more than others. Some will be thought to be better evidence than others for it is quite right for readers to suggest that there might be explanations for what has happened other than the one I personally believe to be true. If anything will not stand questioning it is not worth considering.

The first time my own psychic ability worked in a very unusual way made even me blink. May I say I make no claims to be a great medium and indeed I don't claim to be a medium at all. I have to accept however that in a modest way I am mediumistic. A small group of interested friends were sitting drinking coffee in the home of a gentleman who certainly was a medium. He turned to me and using a phrase often used by mediums asked me 'what I was getting?'. I generally claim that I am never embarrassed in life. I have never been embarrassed by not being able to play the bassoon or fly Concord and I was just about to tell him that I was 'getting nothing' when suddenly I found myself able to turn to another friend and say things which quite astonished me. I was just a trifle embarrassed. I must explain that I had no idea where he had been that day and whilst I knew he was in some kind of engineering and write about him as a friend, he was not an intimate friend and I knew practically nothing about him except that I used to meet him at the home of this medium. I found myself able to tell him with conviction that that day he had been with someone else to a city in Yorkshire to obtain some very important business concession. I told him that he had not gone in his own car, but in a much bigger car. On the way back, I told him he had stopped in a café and there he had had a most unusual experience. I then told him that I was being shown a banknote and described it and its colouring. New £20 notes had been issued but I had not seen one. His face was a study. He reached in his pocket and took out a new £20 note. He told us that he had shown it to nobody and had not even been home before coming to the little group. That day he had gone with his boss to Sheffield on business and they had gone in the boss's car which was a big Rover. On the way back they had stopped for refreshments and had been approached at the table by a man who, excusing himself, had told them that it was his eccentric hobby to single out people from time to time and present them with a banknote and tell them that they could do as they liked with it, but if they invested it in any way, either on a football pool, on dog or horse racing, or put it into the bank or anything which might produce a profit, he put them on their honour to send him a certain percentage. Our friend waved around the £20 note. It was indeed an unusual experience but not as unusual as me being able to tell him about it without knowing from him what had happened. Now you may say that, interesting though this is, it could perhaps be accounted for by mind reading. I can tell you honestly that I cannot read people's minds. I did an act for fun this year, with the local pet shop owner who is a conjuror and it was supposed to be a 'mind reading act'. I was blindfolded and he held up various objects at the church social evening and I then told everyone what kind of an object was held up. In fact I had obtained a list from him of the order in which he was going to hold up various objects which he appeared to have taken from people in the audience at random and I had learned the list in order. No I am not a mind reader. I defy anyone to 'read the mind' of another person as accurately and quickly as the incident in that group so long ago now. The chap with the note had never said a word. Nobody knew what had happened to him that day. I am sure that Paul Daniels whom I greatly admire as an illusionist could conjure up trick after trick which as always could mystify us and which would seem very like what happened to me. But as an honest man he would laugh and without telling us how he did it not deny it was a trick. There was no trick in that group I assure you. Our medium friend had asked me to tell people what I was getting because he could see a man standing beside me. That man, the reader might say, was dead. He was in fact as alive as you and I. Now of course this was a purely material experience. It had no spiritual value except perhaps to start someone thinking, because it was pointing at the person who had given me the message, who by God's Grace had continuation of life. If we have continuation of life surely we must start asking questions about our lives here and on the other side of life in God's plan for us?

The medium friend in whose home we met had a very remarkable gift. We once heard him say that someone on the other side of life was telling him of a disaster in India which would see great floods and a terrible loss of life – it occurred in a matter of days. On another occasion he told us that he could see a large building in Europe in which there were many young people, and he was appalled to see a fire which caused the deaths of dozens of them – this also happened. It was in a cinema in France as I recall. Those things were not pleasant but told to him by those on the other side of life who were concerned to help those who were soon to pass from this world. They obviously had no power to stop those events. I am aware that disasters which are man-made have an obvious explanation but I am also aware that those which are not, raise theological problems. That discussion must wait for another time.

After the incident at the medium's home there then followed a steady trickle of interesting events. I do not accept things easily and in the years of my psychic investigations and experiences I have rejected scores of situations and messages, for, what seemed to me to be, good reasons although I have always tried to be kind to those who felt that they were in touch with people on the other side of life. During the years of my investigations I have had little but extreme kindness from those who possess psychic ability. Only once have I been so cross with a so-called medium that I felt she should be 'drummed out of the union'. If I have appeared persistent and critical I have always found that they understood perfectly and exercised great patience. Among the mediums with whom I have made friends I have found very often great kindness to people in trouble and sometimes I have had genuine admiration for the self-sacrifice to which they have gone on behalf of other people. I may say that also, I have found honesty and willingness to admit that they did not 'get anything' sometimes, when presented with a problem. That fact has also been my experience. Why, we do not always know. Like them I have known what it is like to sit with someone in genuine trouble and be quite unable to latch on to anything helpful. A good medium will not admit to knowledge or information which is not genuine. Mediums are open to the temptation to fabricate and embroider what they see and hear. Any gift has its temptations. A genuine medium of principle will not do either of those things. Of course, as I have pointed out, the only person who is right all the time is God. We expect everyone else in life to make mistakes. Genuine mistakes are understandable. There is considerable danger ahead if the ego of a medium prevents him or her from admitting that mistakes can be made.

I am often asked if messages or communications from the other side of life come in the main from guides. Of course not. Guides appear to be people on that side of life who have been trained for and have the desire for work which is to encourage and help those here on earth. I am sorry to say that in some circles they are regarded with an idolatrous subservience not even afforded the saints of the Church. It must be terribly embarrassing to them to be so regarded and treated. Caligula may have thought of himself as a god. No guide does so and it is quite wrong to approach them in that kind of attitude. It is true also, that in some circles, because the work of guides or helpers is well known that those concerned virtually pray to them. This also is wrong, prayer should be made to God alone. We can talk to guides or helpers and ask for their help and prayers, as we can request the prayers of the saints as we call them. We can feel real affinity with them and experience their love. For me the work of guides or helpers in my own experiences has strengthened my belief in the communion of saints or, as the church puts it, the fellowship of all those here and in the continuation of life who are God's servants. Communication from the other side of life will not always come from guides. Often when possible it will come from ordinary people who have a genuine concern for us. Fun has often been made of the corpus of mediums which is surrounded by exotic guides on the other side of life. However, if you were to know large numbers of mediums, you would discover that those they regard as their guides and helpers, when on earth, came from a complete cross section of all nations. Indeed I can recall one famous medium who was Jewish and she used to laugh and comment on mediums with these exotic helpers. She used to say, 'Do you know who my guide is?' There was always a silence naturally. Then she would say, 'Why, my grandma,' I can tell you that she used to give marvellous evidence of the continuation of life with the help of that grandmother. The question is now clear in your mind; have I a guide or guides? The answer is that I have and whilst all of them are God's servants and devoted to our Lord, not one of them on earth was a member of the Church of England. They appear to be no worse for that, although I dearly love my own branch of the Universal Church.

I recall a very interesting incident many years ago in the bar of my bowling club. I should explain that I have always been addicted to sport. I played rugby and soccer and hockey and cricket and badminton to some effect and enjoyed others with lesser ability. When younger men began to beat me for speed and when I could no longer time the ball on to the bat as well as I once did, I turned to bowls. Bowls is a game at which younger and no longer young men can compete providing the older man has good sight and is fit. It is a game of great skill and now becoming increasingly popular on television. (Here I must boast just a tiny bit and tell you that Tony Allcock, the world outdoor singles champion once only just beat me by one shot in an outdoor club final. Ah me such is greatness!) To return to the story: I was down at my bowling club one night when the club was hosting an evening for blind and partially sighted bowlers. It is quite an education to see these people bowl. They do so by being told according to the mental image of a clock at what time on a clock face the jack and opposing woods lie and they are given the approximate distance of the jack. I am quite sure I couldn't get anything like their results if I closed my eyes and had the same instructions. After the game the club usually puts on refreshments and this was the case and why I was standing in the bar. I thought, as a gesture, I should buy a drink for one of the blind bowlers and I selected one at random, – I had never seen him before in my life. I went up to him and asked him if he would like a pint. The smile on his face told me that he appreciated both the offer and pints generally. We then began to drink our beer and he suddenly said to me, 'Who is that Tibetan standing by you?' It was quite funny really. It was rather like a spy movie in which two agents meet and exchange an intriguing password; 'The ferret is after the rabbit.' or, 'The soloist's G string has snapped.' It just so happened that some weeks before, I had been at home quietly one evening when I had seen quite clearly the figure and face of a man, as clearly as I could see any person I know, except that I was supposedly alone in the room. He was not known to me and he was in the dress of a Llama. A few days later a medium friend described him to me and said he was standing at my side although on that occasion I did not see him myself. I was somewhat surprised at this blind, or nearly blind, bowler coming out with his remark.

'Do you see him?' I asked.

'Yes,' he said quite simply.

'Are you a medium then?' I asked.

He smiled. 'I suppose so,' he said.

I retained his friendship after that until he died a few years ago.

That Tibetan has been to me many times since then. The next time he came, after that incident, he held in his hand a plain wooden cross. It was his way of assuring me that he knew I would have no association with anyone on the other side of life in whom I could not place the utmost confidence because of the dangers of so doing. He was showing me that he was in fact fully accepting

22

the love of God in all that cross stood for and in Him whom it represented. I am aware of course that those who have closed minds on the subject and show bigotry of the worst kind often say that such an incident merely illustrates how devilishly clever the evil ones can be. Of course they can. However to cede the ground to evil so easily merely depicts cynicism of the worst kind. No medium ever sits without first arming himself or herself with prayer to God and by drawing on His Grace through His love and permission so that protection is given. The force of good is always greater than the force of evil, powerful though evil is. The powers of evil assaulted Jesus. They have assaulted every Christian worth the name but we must not unchurch all the good souls doing the work of God on the other side of life through fear or to support some theory or other. Prayer and care are essential and nobody should take mediumistic experiences for granted; nobody should dabble in psychic matters and try to develop without help from a competent God-fearing medium/tutor. Many who think it a great game end up with a nasty shock.

The other people around me from the other side of life have been seen many times by medium friends without collusion. (I mean by that my medium friends who have never met one another to compare notes.) I am most careful not to tell one what another has told me. One of these guides or helpers was one day seen by a friend of mine who did spiritual healing with me and who has some skill in drawing a likeness. This guide had been seen by others but my friend is no medium – his gift lies elsewhere. When I saw the drawing of the man and realised that it was indeed the man described to me by several medium friends, naturally I was interested to know from where he came. He was a Russian Orthodox Bishop when on earth. He told me where he had worked and frankly as it was far from Russia, I tended to be very sceptical. Then one day I was doing some reading and discovered that a long time ago the Russians had colonised that place in large numbers to mine the coal. I have often been told things which seem quite unlikely only to find that in the end they were more realistic than I would have thought possible. This does not prevent me from being rather hard to convince and I hope that will always be so.

23

To illustrate how a guide facilitates information with the other side, I will recount one of my own experiences.

There was, some years ago, a very sad incident in my parish when a young boy was killed when cycling on a busy main road. His parents and young sister were desolate with grief. He was so full of fun and life everyone in the area was stunned. The family were members of another church but I felt I wanted to go round and try to comfort them. I sat and told them of the things I believed and that I was certain that their son was alive and by no means gone from them forever. I shared with them some of the things that have happened to me and the proofs given of the presence of people from the other side of life. This is always a very tense moment for me because it is natural for people to think that if he can receive some communication from a loved one on the other side of life in respect of another person, who not with us? It is a tense moment because sometimes that communication does not come. Occasionally we may offer a reason why this does not happen but no explanation will fit all cases. I am glad to say that as I sat I felt the presence of that boy and with the help of God's servant, my guide, he showed me a pendant and I felt I wanted to put it around his mother's neck and yet take it away. It was hers and yet it was not. I just gave what I was shown and given. It didn't seem much, but her face lit up. She told me the story; apparently at the previous Christmas, the lad had purchased this pendant for his mother. She was of course very pleased but the pendant was not exactly the kind of thing she would have worn by choice. Diplomatically she suggested that he might give it instead to someone else for whom he had to buy a Christmas present and that she would in fact prefer another kind of gift. It was indeed hers and yet I wanted to put it round her neck but I wanted to take it away again. There was no way I could have known about this. They were showing me something about which I had no knowledge. This is the usual way my guide works if possible. It certainly convinced that little family. It didn't relieve the pain of the parting but it gave them hope of the great reunion to come one day. I want to be careful in describing exactly how the pendant incident was transacted by that boy and his mother. There was no rejection of the gift by her and there was great love between them. Mother and son 'came to an arrangement'. The important thing was that the lad was there to tell me about it.

4

The Main Purpose of Mediumship

The main purpose of the psychic faculty as far as I am concerned is to prove, if possible, the continuation of life after life in this world. Some people find that mediums can not only impart to them knowledge about their past but sometimes can inform them of future events in which they are to be concerned. I must say at the outset that this is the area in which most mistakes are made. Some of those mistakes are undoubtedly due to the wrong interpretation by the medium of what is 'seen' or 'heard'. Only God is right all the time. It is far better to deal with someone completely unknown to you, if you are mediumistic. However disciplined you may be it is always a possibility that the mediumistic person will allow prior knowledge about the person they are trying to help to seep into what they are receiving. It is true that often warnings are given and often messages of encouragement about future events which are helpful but as I must repeat, the main task of the Christian psychic is to show that there is continuation of life so that that fact makes a difference to our whole outlook on life. It is not to entertain with knowledge about one's past or forecast the future.

Perhaps I should underline here that very often a medium will not receive information which he or she would like to receive on behalf of someone who seeks help. Why? One explanation which is certainly true is that sometimes the mediumistic person is just out of tune. I am a keen bowler. Often I hear my fellow players who are expert saying, 'Oh dear, (they probably say something stronger than that) I just can't find it tonight.' They are off form. Mediums are often 'off form'. Sometimes nobody is wishing to comment from the other side of life. Often we do not know why this is. People there have free will and sometimes possibly for good reason, and sometimes possibly mistakenly, they refrain from comment. It is true that I rarely sit down to help someone without being aware of our friends on the other side of life but it does happen and sometimes what I pick up is of very little value. Often I just put it to one side as I know how irritating trivialities are to someone who is looking for something concrete. Sometimes I pick up nothing at all. I don't blame those on the other side of life now although I used to do once. It may very well be some fault in me or for some reason of which I am not aware. I can well understand people being critical and thinking that if one can 'see' or 'hear' at all, we should be able to clarify every issue by discussion with guides or helpers. I used to feel that when I first started to 'investigate'. I can only say what seems to be true, which is, that although there are times when the proof given is excellent, there are other times which are very frustrating to both medium and the person they are trying to help. I can only observe that the correctness of what is received so very often indicates that there must be some reason when we do so badly. I am sure that often the fault lies in ourselves.

As far as the honesty of mediums is concerned about what they 'see' or 'hear' it would be a very foolish man who refused to acknowledge those cases where people claiming to be mediumistic have been proved to be frauds or to discount those who are sadly guilty of deluding themselves though not dishonest. I have found sometimes that a person who could have been a good psychic has fallen into the trap of thinking that everything they think is from the other side of life. They are full of imagination. All these people make it much harder for the genuine mediumistic person to be taken seriously. Mediums who write books and cannot recall with accuracy things that have happened in the past then find their book (often written by a ghost writer who can write well enough but who has no real perception of the pitfalls) investigated by a competent journalist who discovers inaccuracies in the book, which are then underlined and so the medium is discredited. None of this does much good for the person who is genuinely seeking the truth and error of it all.

However, whilst I cannot possibly testify to the honesty and integrity of all mediums and the lack of discipline of any given number, I have been very impressed in the past by the integrity of several outstanding mediums. One was facing a full church of people. After some hymns and prayers and an address, this famous medium was to give clairvoyance. People had come from far and wide to hear him. They waited with expectation. He rose and looked at them quizzically and then turning to the conductor of the service asked if a further hymn could be sung. As this was done he sat down quietly. Then he stood up again and said, 'Friends I am very sorry but I am not getting anything at all.' It is sad to record that many people who had been present at a very pleasant and uplifting service quite apart from the clairvoyance were annoyed with him. I know they had come a long way to hear him in many cases but my comment was 'Thank God for an honest man.' On another occasion about which I will write later I was privileged to visit the home of a man with a truly remarkable gift. He was the outstanding 'direct voice' medium of his day. I must explain that term later on and will do so. A small group sat with him of which I was one and be began by saying 'Friends I have had two groups sitting with me this week and I have to tell you frankly that we did not get a thing'. I can disclose at this point that in fact, that afternoon, we had a truly remarkable experience but I was struck initially by the outright honesty of the medium. He promised nothing. Frauds always get something. Indeed however willing to help no medium can promise anything. Nobody in this world has any power over those in the continuation of life. We cannot demand that they attend us. That is why, for instance, the story recorded in the Old Testament in 1 Samuel; 28, verse 3f is incorrect. As I have written, Saul commands the woman at Endor, who was obviously a mediumistic person, to call up the Prophet Samuel. She does so and he appears apparently not in good humour at being disturbed. No medium can call up anybody! If people on the other side of life wish to be present they can do so and if they do not they will not. The great force which does draw people together of course is real love. Love is the tie which binds for eternity. The idea of that woman having any control over God's great Prophet Samuel is ludicrous. One cannot visit a medium and demand to be put in touch with anyone. You can hope that possibly some loved one may be able to be present and sometimes this is so but often it is not and we would have to know the full extent of their activity in the life ahead before pronouncing why. They are certainly not sitting around waiting to be summoned. It doesn't mean that someone you love doesn't care about you anymore. They have their lives to live and work to do and at times no doubt what we are asking is just not possible.

At this point I record another very interesting experience. Some years ago I went to the front door and there stood a young man with his hair down to the navel as was the fashion in those days. He looked at me and said, 'You don't remember me do you?'

I replied that I recognised the face but was searching for a name. He told me his name and I said, 'How long is it since I last saw you?'

'I was about twelve,' he replied. He was then twenty-four and so obviously he had altered rather a bit. I invited him in and he told me a story of graphic interest but which really concerned all the problems and difficulties into which he had drifted. I am not prepared to outline those as they were and are his own personal business. He asked me if I thought that he could get his life sorted out and I said that I was sure that he could providing that he would make the effort and take the advice given. It would not just happen by chance. I described to him a man I saw on the other side of life. He was sitting on a cart according to the picture given to me, and the cart was painted with strong colours and even the spokes of the wheels picked out. I could see the horse in the shafts of the cart but its halter rather hung on it something like a suit of clothes which were too big. The cart was full of junk. This man when on earth I felt sure would buy anything saleable and he always knew where he could dispose of it at a profit. My young visitor recognised him immediately. It was a great uncle who was a Romany. He used to go around with his cart and had a very good eye to business. He had in fact left some money in trust for this young man which he would receive at a certain age. I was then able to say to this young man with the help of his relative who obviously had great affection for him, 'In the not too distant future you will meet a young lady and get married. You will go abroad and financially things will be much better for you. I am told that you will live in Spain or nearby.' Well at that stage he did not think any of it was likely. His reply was, 'Pigs might fly.' One day later he came across another Romany who was a patient in the hospital where the young man had obtained a job as a nursing assistant. This N.A. was a very kindly chap and he took a message from the Romany to a relative living in a caravan just outside the city. On delivering the message he began to talk to the brother of the Romany in hospital and asked him if he could predict things according to the reputation which many Romanies had acquired. This man didn't predict anything but he did say to him that he knew the young man knew a clergyman who was mediumistic (I am sure he didn't use that word) and that he would be advised to 'listen' to him. In itself that was a very interesting thing. In due course this young man met a nurse and, after a whirlwind courtship, married her. Her father was an astute man of business but very anxious to retire and live in Portugal. His plan was to buy a small business there to provide himself with a living in the sun. I had told the young man that he would go abroad in the spring of the next year. I have written elsewhere about the problem of those on the other side of life giving correct time, but in this case it proved correct. Sure enough, in the following spring his new father-in-law bought a small business in Portugal and because he had a son with an incurable disease, he did not want at that moment to leave this country and take the lad away from his doctors. Instead he proposed that his daughter and her new husband should go to Portugal and manage the business until he could take over. The story did not end there. This young man and his wife badly wanted a family. Time went on but this did not occur. They consulted doctors who said that whilst there was no reason why they should not have a family, sometimes it did not work out. (Recent bolder solutions to that problem were not then in vogue.) I told the young man that he would indeed have a child and that it would be born in the following June. He seemed unimpressed in view of the medical uncertainty and their attempts to rectify the situation. One day on a visit from Portugal he visited me and told me that after all I had been given right information from our friend on the other side of life as his wife was pregnant and doctors in Portugal and at home had said she would have a baby in

30

July. 'June,' I said. To cut a long story short they set off from Portugal in June to come to England for the birth of the child in July and the baby was born on the journey – in June. It is not always that our friends on the other side can give time so accurately but it does happen. Medium friends of mine are very reluctant to give time and I have become more and more cautious. It must be very difficult when you live in a state where there is no time, as is the case with our friends on the other side of life, and to break into the time sequences of this world – we hardly know the problems.

I am not in the business of predicting the future as I stress over and over again. It is far more important to me to help people to see that there is continuation of life for all people by God's Love and Grace. The young man had his dramatic proof and few have such proof. What he made of it of course is another, personal, story which has no part of this book. Some who have excellent evidence of the continuation of life think of what that means in God's plan for them and it makes a difference but some do not. This does not surprise me. Jesus taught a parable about a sower who sowed the same seed but it fell on quite different places with different results.

I am aware that so many people who consult a medium for help are not really wanting to establish whether there is continuation of life. Rather they are wanting to know the future. There is a fine line between some prediction with a future content given from the other side to stimulate our thinking about our purpose in life and the future of our own beings, and mere fortune telling. I must stress that it is in the area of future prediction that most mediumistic contributions are wrong. I know one medium who when approached by someone who wants to know purely materialistic things about their future just turns away saying, 'I am not a fortune teller.' In any case when people consult a medium for this reason they are often in the midst of problems which involve other people and with whom they have a close relationship and share problems. Those people have free will. I am not at all satisfied that those on the other side of life see everything that is going to happen to us all the time. They see some things and they are often right when they choose to warn or encourage. Often I feel they just do not know any more than we do. Sometimes they see something on the future pathway of our lives and they assume that other things will therefore follow on the way to that event or state. In other words they deduce very carefully and often cleverly. However, I am sure that they are sometimes wrong in their assumptions, which are given with good intentions, and also they sometimes do not see the whole picture, so that whilst the eventual situation they see may be correct, before that state is reached there are many other events and situations to be gone through brought about often by our own choices and free will. People are annoyed when things they have been told do not take place. One reason is that sometimes the whole pattern has suddenly altered because of free will. On reading this many will feel that it is foolish therefore to expect to be given knowledge of future events and that this should not be pursued. As I say I am not in the prediction business although I have had many experiences of accurate future prediction and of cases where such prediction has helped a great deal to encourage and sustain people. My advice is to take such communications kindly and put them on one side and watch them. No medium worth the name would want anybody to live their lives by consulting mediums. There are those who will not move without doing so. This is very sad and a very foolish thing. Those who do this always in my experience come a cropper. From time to time help is given to us on the pathway of life which is not the pure product of our own thinking and effort. There are various non-psychic ways this can happen. If we do have the good fortune to receive an accurate warning or encouragement about the future, we should take it gladly but not make changes in the efforts we must make ourselves to live our own lives by the intelligence and effort which is expected of us. In any case as I have indicated, these predictions are often out by years and years. I remember once being on a bus, going to town, and I heard two women talking on the seat in front of me very loudly. One of them mentioned the name 'Nella Taylor'. This made me prick up my ears although I am never an eavesdropper but Nella was the medium friend of whom I have written earlier. One woman said, 'She told me a number of things and I waited for them to happen and they didn't and I said to myself, it's all a lot of rubbish. Anyway last week all the things she told me happened and I felt dreadful, having been very sarcastic about her to everyone.' The other woman said, 'How long ago was it that she told you these things?' The reply was, 'Ten years ago,' and she went on, 'I thought originally that it meant that it was going to happen in a few months time.' This is a common experience. I remember one medium friend who was then in the autumn of his life telling me that he had been developed in his mediumistic gift when young by a remarkable medium who had told him a number of things which were to occur on the pathway of his life. Those things had all happened in the last few years and he was now over seventy. Readers have been warned. It is unwise to try to live life by predictions about the future and no good medium would want you to do so. We must use our own intelligence and the ability which God has given to us and ask Him for the strength and help we need from Him through prayer. When recording predictions about the future which have been correct I am not advocating such activity as a way of life, merely, recording facts which are very interesting and to me above all illustrative of the continuation of life because of the presence of those who have passed on the information.

5

Leslie Flint

I said earlier that I would explain the phrase 'direct voice' and record my experience with the medium who was so honest about his recent sittings which were quite unproductive. One day the phone rang and my friend Nella Taylor said, 'I have managed to arrange a sitting with Leslie Flint for one or two friends would you like to come?' Now Leslie Flint had a remarkable gift. He was a 'direct voice' medium. There are others who have this gift but it is generally recognised that, in that particular department, his gift was outstanding. There are various theories about how this gift works. I keep an open mind on that subject. There can be no doubt that if a fraudulent person pretends to clairvoyance or clairaudience, sooner or later he or she will be found out by an intelligent person. After a time it is possible to discern even with people who have a partial gift those things which are the product of their own minds. It is in the sphere of physical mediumship however that fraud has been so easy, due to the credulity of those who come for a sitting . They are so anxious to make some contact with a loved one who has passed into the continuation of life that fraud finds a ready market. For this reason Nella Taylor (like myself) was never very interested in physical phenomena. I remember her once telling me of how she had been present at a sitting and had seen a large nail and a hammer lifted from a dining table and the nail driven into the table by the hammer but with no human hand involved. She had been satisfied that what she saw was genuine. Mrs Taylor had a very sharp and penetrating mind and was not a person whose word I would ever doubt. When she told me about this however my remark was 'I'm glad that it wasn't my dining table.' She laughed. We never failed to see the humorous side of things. She told me once that she went to a meeting where a medium she had long suspected of fraud was supposed to make people materialise in an open cabinet. Knowing she was there, after a time he called her forward saying, 'Nella Taylor this is for you,' rather like the phone advert on television. She rose from her seat and went and peered into the cabinet in which a female form had appeared. 'Who are you?' she asked. 'Why I am your grandmother,' said the so-called person. Nella was very indignant because she hated nonsense and sham. 'Indeed you are not,' she said, and there was consternation in the hall. When she told me this, knowing her and visualising it all, I was just helpless with laughter. We never lost that sense of humour because it was a weapon against rubbish and nonsense. I can remember once seeing her filled with laughter because she had been to a *Psychic News* dinner and I said that I had heard that the waiters could not get around because of the Red Indians and Chinamen in the aisles (a reference to the strange fact that so many mediums claim to have Red Indian or Chinese guides). On another occasion I told her of the chap who went to the home of a famous medium and rang the bell. His housekeeper answered the door, 'Yes?' she asked.

'Is this the home of the famous Mr X, the famous clairvoyant?'

'Yes,' she replied.

'Is it true that he knows everything about the future; great national events and personal happenings to individuals?'

'Oh yes,' she said 'He knows everything – is he expecting you?'

I am telling you these things because when I went to Mr Flint's with Nella, he was admitting to his house two very critical people who hated fraud and nonsense and whose sense of humour was very finely tuned and a potent weapon against deception. There was a good deal of intelligence and knowledge about mediumistic fraud and delusion.

The method of the sitting was this. Mr Flint sat in an armchair, relaxed. At a distance there was a microphone switched on and coupled to an amplifier. He did not move and was in full view all the time. After a short time there was a clear voice through the loudspeaker attached to the microphone. This was his guide who generally chatted with us all and possessed a great sense of humour. It was a normal friendly conversation such as that which friends might engage in on seeing one another. He then introduced several people who spoke clearly and were known to the others there. I remained indifferent because I did not know these people from the other side of life and was not therefore willing to make any judgement as to the accuracy of what they said or about the evidence they gave to prove their authenticity. The only thing which intrigued me was that Mr Flint was able to take part in the conversation in such a way that it was clear that there was no question of ventriloquism. Then suddenly a child's voice said, 'Why haven't you brought my Mummy with you?'

Mrs Taylor gave me a nudge and whispered, 'She is speaking to you Ken.'

Remember, Nella was a great medium and she could see the child. I did not see her just at that moment. I suppose my critical apparatus was working overtime and taking precedence. I thought quickly and replied, 'I don't think so Nella, I don't know a little girl in the continuation of life who would want to talk to me.' Nella insisted, so being a trifle embarrassed I said, 'Who are you dear?'

She replied, 'Patricia.'

It made me jump because I had buried a little girl not long ago and she had suffered from leukaemia. She was a lovely child and I had given her spiritual healing for some time which by God's Grace extended her short life a little and given her parents time to come to terms with the sadness of parting from her. In respect of spiritual healing, which is of course another subject, we all look for complete recovery and sometimes this happens, but often this is not the case and people are helped but in a quite different way to that expected as they journey through life, a journey which is sometimes long in years or very short. This little girl's name was Patricia Jane. Now her parents called her 'Jane' and I used to call her 'Patricia', why I don't know. Nobody in that room knew anything about her except myself. Mrs Taylor had no knowledge of her. One cannot pass on to one's friends all the things that happen to a busy clergyman. Taken aback as I was I was determined to test the situation. I asked her, 'What has happened in your home recently Patricia?'

Her parents had been very distressed, naturally when she died. They were grateful for all that had been done for her and they came to me and asked me if I could tell them whether if they went ahead and had another child, it would be a girl. I always hate these direct questions because I do not claim to be a medium as I have said. However, I was told to tell her that if they went ahead and had another child that they would not be disappointed. That could have been a cover up answer but I don't think it was. In due course they had another child and it was indeed a little girl. The mother had come recently to arrange the baptism with me. This is why I asked Patricia what had happened in her home (the earthly home she had left) recently. Quick as a flash the child replied, 'You mean the new baby? I hope Mummy will not forget me!'

That was good enough for me. Nobody in that room knew these things.

I said, 'No dear she will never forget you or stop loving you.'

'Why didn't you bring Mummy?' said the child.

'I am very sorry dear,' I said, 'if I had known this was going to happen I would have moved heaven and earth to bring her.'

It was a very astonishing experience to hear that child's voice. So far we had had a whole battery of different voices. Even Mike Yarwood would have been hard put to imitate them all.

After a short time in which various people spoke to others a man's voice said, 'Hello Ken.' It sounded familiar but I searched my mind.

'It's Ed Palmer,' he said. 'Cyprus Road.'

Again I was quite surprised. Mr Palmer had been a partner in a firm of well-known painters and decorators which had their place in Cyprus Road. His son had been a good friend of mine and had recently sold the business and retired. His father had been a fine big man and a county swimmer in his day but had been stricken with cancer. One day I was visiting his home in Leicester for he lived in my parish and on going to his room I found him quite close to the end of his earthly life. I went down to the lounge and told his son that his father was dying.

He said, 'I know Ken.'

'I mean that he is dying at this moment Dennis,' I said. 'You had better come with me.' We went up to the bedroom where to cut a long story short I put my arm around his father's shoulder and this very pleasant man passed onwards after a few minutes. We go back now to the sitting with Leslie Flint. I must stress again that nobody in that room knew about Ed Palmer. I had never mentioned him even to Nella. My association with him had been long before I met her or any of her friends. He continued 'I knew that you were there at the end in my bedroom'.

This has always taught me a lesson. People ought to be very careful of things they say when their loved ones are dying and are apparently unable to hear them. Often they do hear them. The inner self is registering. I am sometimes very unhappy about the stark remarks made by people who are unaware that the, supposedly unconscious, person is registering in their inner self through the mind which is still at work. Mr Palmer then went on to mention his children and grand-daughter. The voice was his too. I decided despite all this evidence to test the situation and asked him questions about matters in his family of a personal nature which were known to me and of which it would be quite improper of me to write here. He assured me that in due course a problem which seemed quite insuperable would resolve itself in a way which he outlined. I can only tell you that I passed on this information to my friend, his son, and after a time, exactly what his father had said to me in that sitting at Leslie Flint's house, took place.

It was altogether the most amazing evidence for the continuation of life. For a long time afterwards I asked myself why it was that although I had dear friends and family on the other side of life, these two had come to me, or been allowed to have the time which is obviously limited for sittings cannot go on indefinitely. The power necessary to make it possible wanes after a time rather like an electric current running down. I came to the conclusion that the guides knew that I would be most critical, and if anyone had spoken to me who was known to Mrs Taylor who being a good friend obviously knew a great deal about my background and family and about my friends, with the best will in the world I would have been uneasy and possibly unwilling to accept it clearly. Nobody knew that child or about her and nobody knew about Mr Palmer. I took the point. I had had an experience not given to many for it is the general opinion that although there are other 'direct voice' mediums, few have ever attained his results. Why, we just do not know. In some strange way in his total being he possessed the machinery to make this kind of mediumship possible at this astonishing level. By his own word this did not happen always. I had been very fortunate or perhaps there was some reason why the stops had been pulled out to the full on the other side of life on that occasion. Perhaps someone knew that one day when I was satisfied I would record my experiences in order to help others and that being a canon of the Church I would get a fair hearing and being known as anything but a crank, people would at least read with an open mind.

I am going to be entirely honest with my readers. At that sitting one of the guides spoke to me and urged me to develop my mediumistic ability which was fair enough, but he also then said that he saw a link in this work between myself and another person present in the room, which frankly I doubted although life has often unexpected quirks and takes strange pathways. It was not that I had any objections to working with the person but I knew that person's circumstances and my own and did not see it. It has never happened and I would be most surprised if it did although I am sure that if I ever asked for help with my work from that quarter, and it was possible, it would be given. This raises another point. In the spiritualist church there has grown up a practice which the best mediums deplore, namely, that of thinking that if anything is stated by someone on the other side of life it is like the laws of the Medes and Persians and cannot be broken or treated as wrong. This is of course very silly. As I have written earlier, the only person who is always right is God. No man in any sphere of education, knowledge or learning, or in any aspect or walk of life, humble or great is always right. Sometimes those on the other side of life are quite simply wrong. The greater the mind and more careful the guide the less likelihood of this happening. Like attracts like and the greater the character and integrity of the medium, she or he will be chosen by a guide of exceptional quality as the one through whom they are prepared to exercise their ministry for God. Even so, the greatest guide can be wrong.

I recall the guide of a very famous medium who had given

exceptional evidence and guidance over many years and was very much looked up to as a result. When the 1939–1945 war came along apparently he made a mistake. He had said that there would not be a war at all because nations would not be so foolish again. Mrs Taylor had been prophesying the imminence of a very great and terrible war for several years. It was not a general blanket prophesy which might take care of the next thirty years. She had been saying that it was here now unless nations did something drastic to avert it. This famous guide speaking through his equally famous medium had said the opposite to my friend Mrs Taylor and her guide. I remember being very sceptical about all this at the time and querying whether we could place any reliance in what guides say, when one said one thing and another the opposite. If truth is truth in certain matters they should all be saying the same thing if they could truly see ahead, being out of the physical body. Then after a time I realised the answer. This famous medium, good though she was had fallen into the ego trap. She wanted to be famous for being right and whether wittingly or unwittingly I would not like to say she had offered her own thoughts as those of her guide. It is not possible that a guide of that integrity and known to be so right in the past could have been so mistaken over that particular matter. Let this be a lesson to those interested. We must be on guard against the ego of the medium, but not only that, we must have a margin for the stubborness of some people on the other side of life who just will not come back and say that they have made a mistake. A man who never made a mistake never made anything but some mediums act as if their guides are God himself. This is quite wrong. We have to also judge if what is received is opinion or knowledge. Often guides when asked give opinion. True, often their opinion is better than ours if they have some extra piece of information, being out of the earthly body, which we do not have. Sometimes however they are making a careful judgement on available facts but it can all alter through our own free will and that opinion is wrong. I get a bit fed up hearing mediums always justifying guides' mistakes in a way which suggests that they are incapable of such mistakes. This is nonsense, a good helper on the other side of life will do his or her best. If they are intelligent and careful they will avoid wild guesses and too hasty assessments of situations and sometimes they will be honest and say, 'I don't know.' Several of my medium friends will just simply say to people, 'Friend I just don't know and I am not getting any answer to that problem'. It is possible that it is not intended that they should do so but it is also a fact that often the guides do not know themselves. This sounds as if it is always so unpredictable that what is received is of no value, that is not the case. When it is right it is astounding in its accuracy but it is not always like that. I will give you now if I may two cases, one which was terribly wrong and one which was amazingly right.

The wrong situation came about when someone I know and respected for their mediumistic gift was asked a very important question by someone. It seems that the questioner had a friend who had got into financial difficulties. This friend had asked her to lend her a sum which amounted to the whole of her savings. She wanted to help the friend but was fearful in case the money would not be returned. She wanted to know if when she lent the money it would be returned. The medium, who was in all respects a very good medium and of integrity, I can vouch for that, said, 'Yes, lend the money it will be all right.' She did and the friend got into further difficulties and could not repay it. She lost everything. Now I would never have asked any guide for his opinion in that matter. As a clergyman of experience I would have said, 'If you love your friend enough to possibly lose that money, then lend it; but if not, then do not. It is not a matter for guides but for you. You have free will and must steer your own ship. That is the way God has made you.' Why did the guide slip up? I don't know. I suspect again that in this instance the medium was not in tune or she would have given the answer I would have given without recourse to guides. Perhaps she thought she was receiving the message she gave. I can recall a most wonderful medium, now passed on, who was usually very accurate and gave such accurate messages about time, which is unusual as I have indicated. People used to say that if she told you that you were going to have a great fire in your house at 9.00 a.m. on a certain day, you should have all your furniture on the street at 8.30 a.m. This medium gave me a message she said she had received for me, which was quite wrong. What is the explanation? I suspect again, that she wrongly interpreted what she saw. I am trying here to be honest and trying to avoid a reader thinking that all one has to do is to consult a medium to gain inner knowledge of a coming situation. It may very well be, but often it will not be so.

However, concerning the reverse side of the coin I can record a very interesting situation which I am sure the person concerned will not mind me recounting although naturally again I am not going to record the real name of the person so as to disclose her own personal business. I am not in a court of law proving a case before jury. People must judge whether I am a truthful person or not. This lady however is still alive and would easily verify all I say, were it not for those parts of the account which are her own private concern.

Several years ago a woman rang me to ask if I could see her as she was very depressed. She said that she was not in my parish. I replied that I was there to help people and if I could do so I would. In due course she came and this was her story. Years ago she had been married and then badly let down. She had then lived with her mother and when her mother became ill it was a great blow to her because her mother was not just 'Mother' but a great friend. In due course her mother had died and this had left her very sad and lonely and depressed. She was not an extrovert who rushed about making friends. Above all she wondered if she would ever see her mother again. That was her main concern. Her own friends' views she found unhelpful. I had never seen this woman before in my life and knew nobody who knew her. She was a very pleasant but very gentle soul and as we sat together I went through the usual feeling which I have, of not considering myself a medium like my friend Mrs Taylor and wishing that she had still been alive so that I could have sent the lady on to her, or, wondering if I did not get anything with her, which of my present medium friends would be the best one to help this particular lady.

Fortunately I need not have worried. I was immediately aware of the presence of several people. First there was a man and I was given the picture of him in a greenhouse. He was smoking a pipe. I was told that his greenhouse was a great joy to him on earth and that he came from the Isle of Wight. She then told me that her father came from the Isle of Wight and had obtained a great deal of pleasure from his greenhouse. He showed me the picture of a shop and I was able to describe it and the kind of shop that it was. She told me that that was the shop with which her family had been associated when she was young. I was told the name of a young woman who worked behind the counter at that time and it was correct. They were giving me evidence of their presence by telling me and showing me things about which I had no knowledge – this is quite usual. Then I saw her mother. Naturally I did not say, 'Your mother is here.' Anybody could have said that. I just said, 'There is a lady here,' and described her appearance. Unless there is some distinctive feature about a person this is not always as easy as it sounds. After all people are either tall, medium or small; they are either well-made, to use a kind expression, or of medium build, or thin. Faces fall into a surprisingly small group of possibilities. That is why police photofit experts can quickly get a rough picture from a decent description. Her mother then showed me a necklace and some earrings which when I described them my visitor recognised as those she often wore. I was told that not long before her mother died they had changed the curtains and her mother had sat in bed and, with my visitor, made them up. It had given her mother pleasure. I told the lady that the last holiday that she and her mother had spent together was spent at Bridlington. This was apparently correct. Then the mother on the other side of life outlined to me the problem with which my visitor was faced. As this is of a private nature I would not of course write about it. It was however very accurate indeed and was in many ways the most convincing part of the evidence. From my point of view my main task was to point out to her that I could not know these things unless I was being shown and told and indeed that could not happen unless there was someone there to tell me and show me. The fun-poking question 'Is there anybody there?' was receiving a definite 'Yes' backed with undeniable facts.

The visitor was by this evidence much uplifted and encouraged. After some months she contacted me again and asked if she could come to see me. I replied that she could, but that frankly my experience was that once a person had had such good evidence they rarely got it again. That is not to say that they did not have any further evidence of the continuation of life but it was seldom so convincing. If it was they were fortunate indeed. She said that she would however appreciate the chance to talk to me. She duly came and there were one or two small pieces of evidence offered and then I was shown by a woman, who I knew was her mother, a small coin in mint condition on which was the head of Queen Victoria as a young woman. I took it to be a sovereign or half sovereign. I felt that it was in a small box on a dressing table in the visitor's home but that she did not know about it. She told me that there was such a box. It had belonged to her mother but she said sheepishly, 'I know you will think me funny Canon but I never used to open it. It was my mother's personal box and since her death I have just left it there and still have not opened it.' I said that the best way to verify what was given, was for her to return home and ring me up after having opened the box. In due course the telephone went and it was the lady. 'I have the box Canon,' she said 'I've found a coin with the head of Queen Victoria on it but it is quite dull and it is Queen Victoria as an older woman.' 'No,' I said. 'That will not do, I was shown a coin in mint condition and Queen Victoria as a young woman.' There was a pause and then in excitement she said, 'I've found it.' Archimedes could not have been more delighted. The coin was not a sovereign or half sovereign but a farthing in mint condition. I regard this as a very important bit of evidence as it is one of those small but very accurate things which could not have been dug out of the mind of my visitor, (not that I think the other evidence was dug out of her mind) because she did not know about it. On that same visit I also told her that I was being shown the map of Australia with her, and that towards the back end of the following year she would find that important. She said that she had a cousin out in Australia but she did not know how that was going to affect her. I said that I was told that there were changes coming around her at that time and Australia figured in them. I have seen her since and she tells me that the property in which she had a small business, has had to be sold up, as the proprietor has died and so she is going to retire. This certainly means a change in her life. She has also told me that she has had an invitation from her cousin to visit Australia in a month or two. The rest is her business so to speak but she had indeed had remarkable evidence of the continuation of life from

44

those who care about her. I wish I could do that with everyone. Frankly I cannot nor can any medium. I, like you, often ponder why it is so. It is as if it is just not meant to be. One is tempted to think that it is because there is a 'control' at work; that some need that spur to faith and others are required to exercise faith without that spur. Jesus said, 'Blessed are they that have seen and believe, yet more blessed are they who have not seen and yet believe'. I am being honest about it all and I do not pretend that I know all the answers. I suspect that we shall all know more on the other side of life than we do now.

6

The Undertaker's Proof

One of the most interesting things which has happened to me dates back several years. I have of course, in my time, taken hundreds and hundreds of funerals and have always found the men employed by undertakers as well as undertakers themselves to be very pleasant people and with hardly an exception most kind to those with whom they deal. They are rightly very critical of clergymen who appear 'just to be doing a job' or appear too casual or slipshod, not seeming to care much for the grief of the mourners. I do not think this happens a great deal but it is not unknown. Men drift into the ordained ministry and slip through the screening and become disillusioned. However that is another story. One day I was being driven to a funeral by a young man how said to me, 'Canon I wish I was not working today because my wife is having a baby today and I have just had to turn out because we are so busy. There is nobody else on whom the firm can call.'

I replied, 'Don't worry she will be all right and you will have a daughter.'

He laughed. 'Ah,' he said, 'we know about you but you cannot know that.'

I said, 'Well we'll see,' and the subject was changed.

Some weeks later he was driving me again. 'We did have a daughter,' he said, 'and my wife was all right.' It was my turn to laugh.

I said, 'Well there are boys and girls. I had a fifty fifty chance.'

He replied, 'True but you knew didn't you Canon?'

I said, 'Yes on that occasion I did know but I hope I am not going to be pressed into service to sex the babies of expectant mothers because more often than not I am not told at all.'

He then went on to say, 'Would you see a friend of mine who has had a very terrible experience? He has lost a small child.'

I replied that I would as long as the man whom I had never met came to me as to a minister willing to comfort and help but that I could not guarantee to obtain psychic information at will and often did not do so.

He nodded. 'That is honest,' he said.

In due course this man came to see me. He had paid a visit with his small daughter and the children had gone upstairs to play. There had been a window which was not correctly latched and his child had in some way leant against the window, probably climbed on something to play, and had gone out of the window and had been killed. It was tragic. The man was desolate. I said to him, 'If I said to you that your daughter was here and she was saying "Daddy" you would think and say, "What a load of rubbish, even the postman could say that".'

He said, 'Well, I might not have said it vicar but I would have thought it.'

'I know,' I said, 'and so I will not do so. Instead, I want to tell you that I am being shown the map of the middle of the country, and I want to go over the border of Shropshire into Wales and there, there was a woman called Agnes who brought you up.'

He sat bolt upright on his chair. 'How do you know that?' he said.

'Is it true?' I asked.

'Yes,' he replied. 'During the war. We were evacuated as children to Welshpool and that woman Agnes looked after us. I am astounded vicar. How do you know?'

'Only if someone is telling me,' I said. 'And if someone is telling me there must be someone here to tell me, friend.' I went on, 'She is telling me that she was very strict, and though she was kind, she did not want you to go back home for your parents to think that you had been allowed to do just as you liked.'

'That is quite true,' he said. 'She was a fine woman and we were most grateful to her.'

'Then,' I said, 'also there is another woman here; this is an aunt of yours and she lived in a village. She too was a wonderful

47

person. If anyone in the village was ill they sent for her. If anyone had to be laid out as they say, people sent for her. If there was a baby to be born, they sent for her and in fact if anyone wanted to borrow half a pound of margarine it was to her they went.'

'That also is true,' he said.

'And,' I went on, 'she had a stroke at the end of her life and ended her days, sadly, in a wheelchair as she was paralysed.'

'I am amazed, vicar,' he said. 'How can you know?'

'Only if there is someone here to tell me,' I replied. 'Now the point of this evidence is this. If you had to pick two women to bring up your child; could you pick two more wonderful women than those?'

'No,' he said. 'Why, vicar?'

'Because,' I said, 'your child will not stay a child forever. That would be very silly. God is not a fool. When children pass prematurely into the next sphere of life, they do not grow to old age, but they grow to maturity. Your child needs those who will look after her in this new stage of her life and these two women have been asked if they will undertake the task and they have agreed.'

His face was a study. He said, 'You've given me something to think about vicar and I feel much encouraged and feel better for it.'

Off he went. Some months afterwards he came back.

He said, 'I have been checking up on you vicar.'

'Oh,' I replied 'How?'

'Well,' he said, 'I have not kept up writing to that woman Agnes as I should have done. You know how things are. You should do things but you get slack, especially over letter writing. To be honest my conscience has been pricked. I have made enquiries and I have found that she in fact died almost a year ago.'

'Oh yes,' I said, 'She is on the other side all right, like the man who is standing by you now. Since you last saw him he has been killed in a car accident but when you were with him last it was in Germany and you were driving Centurion tanks together'. His face again was a study. 'Is that true? Did you drive Centurion tanks in Germany?' I asked.

'Yes,' he said, 'I did.'

That man needed a spur to faith. I have not seen him since but I felt he had had an experience which would in the long run be very important to him on the pathway he was treading. Sometimes the evidence given is dramatic and sometimes very little. The important thing is that it should be accurate and something the mediumistic person did not know and could not know. In my experience one has periods of being in tune and receiving a number of things over a short time which are accurate and helpful. Then there are lean periods in which you begin to wonder if the gift has left you. So often when that happens, off you go again almost as a proof to yourself that it has its place in the scheme of things.

In recent years there has been a renewed interest in the Church's ministry of healing. Spiritual healing has been a part of the ministry in my church for over twenty years. I remember once Bishop Williams of Leicester who was a fine scholar and a man of very quick perception and intellect gently telling me about a silly remark that had been made to him about the healing at St Peter's. I was the Bishop's editor and in fact served in this capacity for twenty-four years. During this time I was aware that my outspokenness on all kinds of subjects and a natural flare for journalism aroused the ire of those in the diocese who did not agree with what I wrote. Some, who had not the courage to contest what I wrote and probably felt that they had no case anyway, thought that they could unsaddle me by going behind my back and complaining to the Bishop. Ronald Williams never fell for such tactics. He was aware that I wrote impartially on all subjects because I belonged to no party inside or outside the church. Even though Ronald Ralph might not entirely agree with me, he defended my right as editor to write without in any way being controlled by people with vested interests, or by some, whom I am sorry to say were jealous of the privilege I had of writing where many read. The local newspaper *The Leicester Mercury* almost inevitably 'lifted' my editorial (with permission of course). Bishop Williams would often go through with me some public announcement he proposed to make, or some speech in the Church Assembly or the House of Lords, because he knew that my feet were always on the ground and that I would spot some unfortunate word or phrase, and that, living life at grass roots, I would honestly tell him the kind of reaction I felt his words would receive in different quarters. I greatly valued this confidence and he used to say to me that the time we spent each month going over, world, national and local issues was most valuable. He was a fine Bishop and gave leadership sadly lacking today and he commanded respect in London as an elder statesman. I was also fortunate during my editorship in having this backing for my independence from the Venerable Harold Lockley, the Archdeacon of Loughborough, another gifted and able man who saw the value of what I was doing. All that is in passing! The Bishop, as I have written, with some small embarrassment mentioned this silly remark about the healing at St Peter's, saying that someone had rung him and asked him if he knew that in St Peter's 'spirits' were seen floating about the church. I could not contain my merriment and I am sure that he felt that he ought never to have brought up the matter. Later I produced a copy of the short service which we used when there was a service of spiritual healing in church in which it is made very evident that healing is asked from and offered solely in the name of Jesus Christ. I asked him, of course, to attend one of the services and to take part. I also mentioned that St Paul (or possibly another Christian writer) said that, 'we are compassed about by a great cloud of witnesses'. I wasn't aware of any spirits 'floating' about in St Peter's but I understood that we believed that those who stood for God's truth and were servants of Jesus Christ were continually attended by those who had 'died in faith' and lived to praise God and continue to extend his kingdom and therefore to help us. He agreed. I don't know how he replied to the silly man who complained. Knowing him he might well have said, 'The report of floating spirits in St Peter's is greatly exaggerated. I have attended that church many times and never seen one, all spirits being confined to the Vicar's sideboard especially after Christmas presents have been received, after which there is a sad dearth of such until next Christmas.' He never did tell me what he replied.

Bishop Williams did of course seriously talk with me about whether we could rely on the evidence offered by mediumistic people. He said that he had never had such experiences and as a scholar could not therefore pronounce on their validity. He had been my principal at theological college and had had a long time to decide whether I was a true scholar or a fanciful person. The fact that I felt that the whole subject was worthy of study weighed with him. I told him that I thought that it was unfortunate that the Church had not done an in-depth study of the whole range of psychic activity under the guidance and leadership of someone who knew all the pitfalls and was devoted to the truth, fact, and honest appraisal but free from the anti-mediumistic prejudice that ruins most attempts at a correct evaluation. He thought such a study was probably worthwhile but was not in an area in which he was prepared to launch out.

I am sometimes asked by people if I am aware that the police have been known to obtain help from mediumistic people and of course I am aware of this. Sometimes the police have shown a willingness to consult a medium in the hope that he or she may pick up some fact that will lead them to a result. A medium known to me was living in a village where there was a rather nasty murder. The police naturally visited every house and on coming to her said that they were aware that she was a medium and asked if she could give them any help. Her reply was that she could only give what she picked up. She said that the man responsible would kill again before they caught him and would attempt a third victim but would fail and because of this they would catch him. Of course I am aware that objectors will ask why whoever gave the medium that message did not somehow give information which would have prevented the second murder? Frankly I do not know and I am not going to guess or to pretend to knowledge that I do not have. One can only speculate the answer. In some circles it is believed that those on the other side of life who act as guides have almost unlimited powers. I believe that this is fanciful. That they do help us I am quite sure. However, all of us have free will, even deranged and wicked people. It is possible that those on the other side of life see the pattern of events without having the power to alter that pattern very often. They can guide and help by thought projection but are not infallible. I believe that only by prayer to God and God alone can events be altered. The subject of whether prayer works and whether God intervenes of course is the subject for another piece of writing. Christians down the centuries would say that they are aware that prayer is answered although not always as we wish it to be.

The reader will allow me, I am sure, one or two diversions of this character to show that I am aware of the issues and problems raised by claims that the psychic has a useful purpose in the proper hands.

I am more than grateful for the long hours of discussion I had many years ago with Mrs Taylor and her great patience with me and the patience of her guides. One of those friends used to say, 'If a thing will not stand the test of the reason God has given, it is of no value.' If I ever become so critical that I placed her in a position where her back was against the wall trying to deal with my hyper-critical objections, she never wriggled out of the situation with a platitude or piece of verbal nonsense. She was not frightened to say, 'I don't know but there is an answer and we must find it.' Often we did.

Before taking up the story of further experiences I must record the astonishing story of how Mrs Taylor met up with one of her two main helpers on the other side of life. Nella Taylor was married to a police sergeant who had no time for nonsense and we must remember that we are talking of a time when there was perhaps little sympathy for mediumistic persons. It was not so much a question of regarding them as witches and calling for their burning at the stake, but previously there had been a period in which a good deal of fraud and nonsense had been unearthed. Even Sir Oliver Lodge, a most reputable scientist and I am told very respected in his day, had been completely deceived by a medium and had strangely continued to believe in him after he had been shown to be a charlatan. Mrs Taylor therefore was allied to a gentleman who was not sympathetic to frauds and cheats. When I was a boy I had a great friend, old enough to be my father, who was like an uncle to me. He too was a policeman, a great runner and a wrestler in his day. When I was a young man I once told him of an encounter I had had with a mediumistic person who had told me of two most important things that would occur in my life. Both of these 'predictions' turned out to be correct, although I had neither met him before, nor knew of any mutual acquaintance. My friend dismissed my story with contempt, saying, 'I lock up people like him.' I am mentioning this because Nella's husband was disinclined to believe rubbish and that is the understatement of the year. Nella had always had this psychic ability since childhood and her remarks had often caused some perturbation for her mother. One such occasion was when the vicar's wife called and in the course of the visit, the tiny Nella had asked, 'Why has she got two faces?'

'Whatever do you mean?' asked the outraged lady.

'She has two faces,' said Nella. 'One on the front and the other on the back.'

Apparently this was a fair comment on the character of this woman who was well known locally. The response was, 'You are going to have trouble with her,' and the lady of the manse swept acidly away.

One evening Nella was sitting in her home with a friend and her husband was away on duty. As far as she was concerned then she just dozed off. When she 'awoke' her friend was excited and very agitated.

'What's the matter?' asked Nella.

'You seemed to doze off,' said her friend, 'then after a time a woman's voice with a broad Yorkshire accent seemed to come from you. I was quite astounded and disturbed.'

Nella Taylor by the way was a Derbyshire woman. She laughed and thought that her friend was pulling her leg. However it was soon clear that this was not so nor was the friend psychologically disturbed, nor had she been drinking.

'The voice of the person,' said her friend, 'said that we must sit down tomorrow night and we then would find out more.' Nella was convinced that it was a joke. The next evening they were sitting together and the friend plucked up courage to ask Nella to just relax and see what happened. Dismissing it as a lark Nella just relaxed without thinking anything might occur. Sure enough she went into what later she knew was a trance and the voice of a Yorkshire woman with an accent that you could cut with a knife seemed to come from her and make a certain request. On becoming fully awake again Nella was told by her friend that the woman who had spoken through her had requested that they visited the races at Pontefract and there they would find a Gipsy Caravan coloured in a certain way and an old boot hanging in the window, with a young Gipsy woman sitting on the steps. That young woman would take the matter a step further. Well, frankly Nella was sceptical despite her own psychic experiences. She had no fear. She was a devoutly brought up Anglican with a great trust in God. All her life she distrusted psychic phenomena looking for any obvious manipulation although like me if she found a situation to be genuine she never lacked the courage to say so.

Her friend was by now astonished and keen to see if what had happened had any substance. Of such are pioneers and explorers made. She worked on Nella to go with her to the races and see if they could find this caravan. Nella was not convinced but she said that she would consider it, although she made her friend promise not to tell her husband who, as I have said, was quite likely to explode with indignation. In any case those were different days and ladies did not go to the race tracks unattended. Strange it was that when he came home from his police shift he told Nella that the next day he and some men had been detailed off to go as a special detail to the Pontefract Races. As far as Nella was concerned this killed the whole idea of her going with her friend. Her husband would never agree to her going and certainly not on such a fanciful project. The next day early her husband set off for the races. Her friend came round armed with a bus timetable and a very persuasive voice. 'I have looked at the times of the buses,' she said. 'We can go on this one and return on that.'

'Tom will never agree,' said Nella.

'Tom need not know,' said her friend now thoroughly caught up in the adventure. 'Besides there will be so many people we won't see him.'

There was a long argument and then Nella gave in. They caught the bus to the races. They spent several weary hours wandering about looking for the caravan which was nowhere to be seen. In fact Nella was feeling tired and dejected when she saw her husband and another policeman in the distance. She crouched down behind a bookie's stand.

'Ay Missis,' he said, 'wot yer doing?'

'I don't want to meet that policeman,' said Nella.

54

'Why wot yer bin doin'?' asked the bookie. 'I don't want a brush wi' the law.'

'It is my husband,' said Nella.

'Blimey,' he said, 'that's torn it lady. I'm favourite to be run in.'

In some way Tom was so occupied with other situations that he failed to see Nella who by now was almost a nervous wreck. Dejectedly they decided to return to their home before they were seen by Tom. In any case they had to get back before him so as not to have to say that they had been there at all. Then her friend noticed a clump of trees.

'Just one more look Nella,' she said and propelled the reluctant Nella around this clump of trees behind which they had not looked. To their astonishment there was the caravan. The colours were right, the old boot hung in the window and on the steps was a young Gipsy woman smoking a pipe. They approached her nervously. The young woman looked at them.

'It's taken yer all yer time,' she said. 'Ah thowt ye would never come.' The young woman went on to tell them that she was aware that her grandmother whom we would call 'deceased' had informed her that she had spoken to Nella and her friend and that she wanted Nella to know that if she would have her, she would come regularly to her and operate a ministry of help and guidance to other people which would in time make Nella famous in more countries than her own. Naturally when they had swallowed hard and asked what she meant by 'come to Nella,' they enquired why this old Yorkshire Gipsy woman on the other side of life should attach herself to Nella when the woman obviously had relatives to whom she could go. The young Gipsy told them that in her clan or tribe when someone like her grandmother died, all her goods and her caravan were burned to avoid jealousy among her survivors. If she worked with one of them it would cause resentment. Nella had been selected by her for this work if she would do it. It was entirely up to her. No doubt the local vicar would have wrung his hands in horror and told her to go back and wash and iron and cook and say her prayers. Had she done so hundreds and hundreds of people, I could not hope to compute the number, would have been deprived of real evidence of survival after physical death which changed their whole thinking about God and his purpose

55

for them. Her vicar might have felt they should arrive at their understanding of God's free gift of Eternal Life through Jesus Christ, which was how Nella always put it and how I always put it, in some other way, but then as Nella would often quote, 'God moves in a mysterious way His wonders to perform and He is no respector of persons' and might have added, 'nor of clergymen and their narrowly conceived views.'

Perhaps I should say something about the word 'selected' which I have used about Nella Taylor's work in co-operation with the woman who on earth we would have called a Yorkshire Gipsy. It is obvious that Nella was born with this great gift and it was obvious to her husband, as I say a police sergeant, that that gift ought to be used correctly. Once reconciled to it he told her that it must not be played with and must be used in the right way. In due course she came under the tutelage of a medium who had the gift of developing the gift in others, or, as we would call him, a teaching medium. There are few of these about who are really genuine teaching mediums. There are those who attempt to 'bring on' others with a psychic gift. They have some success but first-class teaching mediums with enough expertise to deal with all the many facets of mediumship and the individual aspects of each person concerned are few and far between. There came the day when Nella's teacher had to say to her that he could in fact teach her no more and indeed in due course she surpassed him. Those on the other side of life who have the ability to serve as guides obviously train for it and they have free will there just as they had free will here.

Sally, the Yorkshire Gipsy woman who attached herself to Nella Taylor had watched Nella and decided that she was the kind of person with whom she wished to work. Again it depended on Nella and her own free will. There was no question of her being taken over. It was a kind of partnership. Together they helped a very large number of people over many years. Sally was a real character and her asides during those moments when she was working with Nella in trance were often hilarious. At the same time she was most down to earth. On the whole apart from certain pithy Yorkshire sayings she did not use torrents of words which sounded well but said very little on analysis. She was quick to come straight to the heart of the matter and her blunt manner may not always have been to the liking of those who wished to hear from the other side of life what they wanted to hear. Sally spoke the truth as she saw it. Anybody who wanted something different was disappointed.

Mrs Taylor was a very fine trance medium. Those who are used to the parodies on mediums in trance usually seen in television plays and on films would soon have altered their view had they ever had the privilege of sitting with Nella when she allowed one of her two main guides to speak through her in trance. I have spoken for hours and hours, not all on the same occasion of course, with both of these guides. I am quite satisfied that the situation was genuine. I was highly honoured, for Nella did not allow this privilege to many. She dealt with people normally by common sense and experience, by her recourse to Scripture and honest religion as some might term it, and by using her clairvoyant and clairaudient powers or gifts.

The other guide who mainly worked with her was a man who had lived in China. I possess a small silver spoon given to me by Mrs Taylor, one of a set given to her by a friend (as she became) who had been a matron on a hospital ship stationed in the Far East. This matron had met Nella and in due course had been allowed to speak to her guides when Nella was in trance. By now of course the nurse had retired to this country. To her astonishment the man from China had spoken to her in detail about parts of China that the matron knew well and they were able to have a normal to and fro conversation about them. In all respects he was most accurate and his Chinese naturally perfect. Nella had never been to the Far East and knew no Chinese dialect, although the matron had learned Chinese.

The contrasting difference between these two guides was quite amusing. Sally, a Yorkshire woman with her broad accent and the man from China, scholarly, highly intelligent, a great philosopher, with a mind as sharp as a needle and stored with quotations as much from Christian Scripture as from other sources.

I ought to mention something about trance mediumship. Now at first I admit I did not particularly like the idea. We are our own persons and I am known for being very outspoken and independent. I would not surrender that to some other human being, even for a short time, unless I was very sure it was right and proper. I have seen mediums go into trance and frankly have been far from satisfied with the result. This is because I have had the experience with Nella Taylor of seeing a real medium with a great gift, consecrated to God, allowing herself to be entranced to help others. Mrs Taylor would take perhaps ten minutes to become entranced. I have seen other mediums appear to be entranced in seconds. Later on when I knew more than I did in the first days of my investigations I realised that they were not really in trance at all. In some cases, where I would want to be kind, they were in a kind of light trance. This is possible and the medium can hear the guide working through him or her, as it seems, in the distance, but it is not a genuine deep trance. In light trance there is always the chance that the mind of the medium may interfere with the words of the guide. Of course this is also true of clairvoyance an clairaudience. Each statement from the other side of life needs to be proved correct.

The man from China who was Mrs Taylor's guardian, if I may put it like that, used to say to me occasionally when she was really deeply in trance, 'You can stick a pin in her if you wish.' The idea of sticking pins in my dear friend did not appeal to me but there was no doubt that she could not have felt it if I had done. In any case I was far more interested in the truth of what was said through her, than in such physical games. I once asked her guide what happened when he took over in trance. He said, 'It is hard for me to explain and you will know when you come to this side of life, but I turn off her mind.' What that means I do not know. All I can tell you is that when she returned to full control of her own powers she knew nothing at all of what she had said in trance. It was quite useless to back track and try to clarify something said by the guide, expecting her to know about it for she did not.

I have mentioned my experience with Leslie Flint and I have of course had other experiences quite apart from that and many such with Mrs Taylor in which the medium was in trance. It is very interesting. I do not now pursue such experiences as I feel I have been allowed to see and hear them and I am not obsessed by this kind of mediumship or physical mediumship of any kind as some apparently are. People have to live their lives in this world according to the abilities God has given them. I am quite sure there is nothing wrong with those on the other side of life assisting people here along their pathway in the same way that they would if they too were here still on earth. They use the means open to them to do that.

Whilst on the subject of trance I must say that I am not myself in any way desirous of acquiring this ability or developing it. After all we cannot have the vicar going into a trance. That would indeed invite some sarcastic comments. I prefer to be alert and to be able to use my own wit and sense of humour for which I am well known, on my critics. I have however in my time attended two very remarkable meetings for the occasion of mediumship known as 'transfiguration'. It is not a word I like because being a Christian minister that word is for me associated with the occasion described in the gospels when Peter, James and John had also a very remarkable experience. They had been taken quietly out of the village or town by Jesus for meditation and prayer and suddenly he was filled with a Divine light so that his whole being and person seemed alight and the account says that there appeared to him Moses and Elijah; Moses representing the teaching of the Jewish Law and Elijah representing the prophetic voice of those great servants of God spoken of in the books we call our Old Testament. The three disciples were astonished but the occasion was such that they tried to perpetuate it by making the spot a Holy Spot with shrines which could be revisited. Only when I came to know what I now know about mediumship did I fully realise what happened on that spot long ago and came to accept truly that the presence of Moses and Elijah with Jesus was not only possible but quite normal, for people from the other side of life are present with us continually and sometimes seen and heard by those with the ability to see and hear them.

The first occasion I experienced this type of mediumship was many years ago when Harold Baxter came to Leicester. I was persuaded to go to this meeting not expecting much and being very sceptical about physical mediumship and hyper-critical about psychic things just at that time although I realised that there was more to it all than I had been prepared to admit. Mr Baxter explained to the meeting what was to happen, and then sat in a chair in a darkened room lit only by infra-red lamps. He explained that ectoplasm was used in the type of mediumship in question and that it was destroyed by daylight. I am not an expert on ectoplasm but I understand that it has been photographed with special cameras and lighting especially in the USA where investigations into psychic things are far in advance of investigations here. I am aware by the way that there have been many fraudulent photographs, purporting to show ectoplasm which has simply been muslin. Ectoplasm seems to be a substance which certain people are capable of producing from the mouth and nose on which those on the other side of life can imprint a form – laugh away my friends. Some reading this book will no doubt at this stage have decided that the poor old canon despite his Honours Degree in Theology, a distinction in his Diploma in Theology and subsequent M.A. and Doctorate in Philosophy, has become quite potty! I expect that Darwin felt that when he wrote his great book based on his observations of natural life that there would be many who would scoff and call him a lunatic. There were, but we are glad that he had the courage to describe what he saw and make some attempt to evaluate it.

In due course the face of Mr Baxter took on another form. It was as though his features, being made of rubber had been remoulded and the voice that accompanied his new personality matched the features. Frankly I was quite surprised. Even more was I surprised when person after person superimposed their features on his and spoke to those in the meeting who knew them. It was quite astonishing. Mike Yarwood is able, after hours of make-up, to present different faces to us and voices too for entertainment and has the knack of making his face look like some famous person we know. He cannot however without any prior association with people in the audience mimic their relatives who have passed into the world beyond ours. All the people who came from the other side of life were recognised and had a running conversation with family and friends in the audience which could only have been fraudulently carried off, for it was so normal and perfect on both sides, by professional actors both in the world of spirit and in the audience who had learned their lines. One person who came through was an old lady with a most delightful personality and full of fun who after engaging relatives in a most intriguing conversation containing scores of references to people and places and events, then roguishly declared that as she was 'in control', meaning that she had been schooled into how to operate through Mr Baxter by his guides, she was not going to withdraw. She did of course. Another was a child and the face of the child was quite distinct and the voice as well and the obvious delight and amazement of the child's parents who were in the room was stunning. I am fully aware that attempts at this kind of mediumship are not always attended by such success and I have heard of occasions which have not been 'on the ball'. As I am never tired of saying, cars break down, scalpels are not sharpened sufficiently and cause wrath in the operating theatre, electrical devices fail, the Space Shuttle blows up, Chernobyl hits a whole continent. Only God is perfect. Sometimes we expect too much. I know we have to be very careful over psychic things and so I am. I have no time for nonsense. I am fully aware of the phenomena of mass hypnosis and hysteria and so on. However, I must say that I am satisfied that what I saw and heard at that meeting with Mr Baxter was genuine. I shall probably never see the like again. It is a pity more who decry the possibility of such things could not have had the same experience. I know that Harold Baxter's gift was an outstanding one. Why he should have that gift in greater measure than others I don't know. However it follows the human pattern. Pavaroti has a voice which edges out other great tenors. Moira Anderson's lovely voice is not however like Mirella Freni's great voice. Baxter had a great gift. I am glad I saw it in action. I also had a very interesting experience when I attended similar kind of mediumship through Mrs Nixon. Again the evidence was remarkable and I would say genuine although not quite so dramatic as that I have described in the meeting with Harold Baxter. I am aware that some people would feel that what I have described could easily be faked with care by those who had a mind to do so. I am sure it could providing that there was collaboration between the illusionist/impressionist and the people in the audience. However there is no such person who can just come into a room and perform a trick of that nature without preparation and collaboration. The secret of great illusionists like 'Dante' whom I loved to see as a boy is to make it all look so natural and easy but any honest illusionist would say with a grin that of course you must work out how it is done and he means that he is taking you for a ride but that is his living and he is not revealing his secrets. It has been known that some mediums in the past have tried to keep up a reputation when their powers have waned by inserting material which is not genuine, if I may put it like that. The human ego is subject to pride. We must always be watching for this kind of thing. The honest medium who is a God-fearing person will readily admit when things are not right and will not mind saying that they cannot, for some reason, either known or unknown, get it right on that occasion. Many of you may feel it is all too much of a struggle sorting it out. I can sympathise with that feeling. However what I am trying to do in this book is to share experiences with you and to establish that it is possible to make contact with those who have passed into the world beyond our present earth world. Also to say that this contact is not evil as some would have us think. Why some think that father and mother who have been wonderful people and much loved are wrong to make a contact with us from the other side of life I can't think. To me they are as welcome now as ever. Physical death does not change love.

It is always intriguing when some piece of evidence is given which shows precognition of knowledge of the future and this is often so. As I have said it sometimes has the unfortunate result of making the recipient thirst after continued messages of a similar character. Before critics condemn that as a very low standard of experience without any value to the progress of the soul, I must point out that this is well understood by a medium of spiritual worth. Mediums who are essentially interested in the growth of the soul and mind in spiritual advancement soon put material messages about earthly future events into perspective and only really see those as either an arrow shaft to point to the really important aspects of progress, or as a means of guiding someone on to a necessary pathway or through some great problem so that better things can be reached. There may well be materialistic mediums who have very uninspired contacts from the other side of life who just use their psychic gift to entertain or mystify or assist in materialistic situations. My own experience is that those who do this sooner or later give wrong advice and cause great disappointment and even distress. A good spiritually orientated medium will always couple any materialistic help with some spiritual advice which in the long run is the main consideration. I have to say it, and this is not an attack on clergymen of whom I am of course one, but Nella Taylor helped more people during a month than most clergymen can hope to do in a year. She was always most humble, never arrogant and I am always critical and distrustful of purely materialistic mediums who use the psychic gift for their own aggrandisement and fame. With her, God came first and last. She was, she said, 'only an instrument of His'. With this attitude I agree wholeheartedly.

Future prediction is not wrong if it serves a purpose. It is however, the area in which most mediums bare their Achilles' heel. Perhaps there is too often the desire to be shown to be right and the boost to the ego of being thought to know things which others do not.

I had a very interesting experience one day after receiving a telephone call from a lady not far from Leicester who lived in a delightful part of the county. She had, a little time ago, lost her husband by death and as she had loved him dearly and they had been together for a very long time, she was now very sad and very lonely. She was a God-fearing woman and she believed that her husband had continuation of life but this did not quench her inner sorrow. Someone had told her to go and see me. Now I am always somewhat uneasy when this happens as I make no claims to be a medium and my main work is the solidly orthodox work of a clergyman. Part of that of course is comforting people. I tend to point this out to people and to comfort them in terms of faith and trust and only to employ any psychic contact if indeed it begins to work without trying to harness it. I happened to be driving one day close to this woman's home and so I said that I would call in and see her as she was elderly and had no car.

I little thought when I visited her we should find such evidence given of the continuation of life. I began by talking to her about her husband and asking about his passing, as I had never met him or her nor knew anyone who knew them. As we talked suddenly he was there. Now I never say to anyone, 'Your husband is here.' Anyone can say that. It is not evidence. Very quickly in a completely strange house he told me a number of small things which set the scene. I defy anyone who talks glibly of telepathy to come into my house and pick my mind accurately and with speed, as fast as I can talk. But with that speed I was able to tell her that her husband sat in a certain chair which was correct, I was able to tell her that he loved a glass of whisky at nighttime. This was also correct and she hastened to add that the doctor had in fact recommended this. I know hundreds of people who do not drink spirits. I did not go upstairs in this house which I had never visited but I was able to tell her because I was told by him on which side of the bed the reading lamp stood, on which side of the bed he had slept and of the combination open to people of using a pillow and bolster, several pillows or just one, which selection he had favoured. He told me of their last holiday together in Cornwall and how they had stood at Lands End, like so many holiday-makers, right at the tip of the country. He then showed me a watch and a waistcoat and talked of having a waistcoat made with a suit which many men do not do today, so that he could wear this watch which he valued greatly. This was also correct. The watch had been given to him by his father. He told me to tell the lady that sometime ahead she would read something in a newspaper which would be to her benefit and surprise her. On this I could get no more from him than a chuckle. However the lady was convinced that there certainly was a contact with her husband and I myself had no doubt of it. The story does not end there for some months afterwards she rang me in great excitement to say that one day she had been at the home of a friend and had idly picked up a newspaper which contained the stock market and other prices. A very long time ago she and her husband had bought an interest in which she had taken no part and had never given the matter another thought leaving such things to him. Indeed she had forgotten all about it. She just suddenly felt compelled to look down the column and the name of the investment caught her eye. Intelligently she was aware of the vast increase in value since those days long ago when her husband had first mentioned the matter and she followed it up. She found the documents which he had filed away and discovered the present value of the investment which was indeed a most pleasant surprise as he had told her it would be. Quite obviously it was not possible for me to know about this without being told by him.

Now of course this did not make her a Christian believer; she was already a believer. It did not cause her to believe in God's gift of Eternal Life. She believed in that although she confessed honestly that she had had qualms after her husband's death such as might come to everyone faced with that crisis. This experience had however convinced her and helped her immensely as she journeyed on along the remaining part of her own earthly pathway. For her it was a necessary experience. Why she should be granted this and such an experience not granted to everyone faced with such loneliness I cannot tell you. All I can do is record the event. Some time afterwards she rang again and said that she had the chance to see a medium and did I think it would be all right. I said, 'Of course but do not expect too much. You have had a remarkable experience not granted to many. It is now a case of having faith and trusting God.'

She replied, 'Yes I agree but if you tell me not to see the person I will not do so.'

I replied, 'It is not for me to tell you what to do in life but for you to do as you feel you should.'

She saw the medium and rang me again. 'I am afraid the medium did not get very much,' she said. 'She seemed to be groping around, nothing like the evidence you gave me.'

'That is because she was trying to help you, but the truth is that you have had your evidence and must now make your way in faith,' I said. She accepted it. As I pointed out hundreds would be delighted to have had her experience and have had the evidence she had been given. It was, as you will have noticed, evidence of the presence of a loved one but also containing as evidence some knowledge of the future for her husband knew she would rediscover that holding some months ahead, in a very unusual way.

7

The Whole Company of Heaven

On the other side of life it must be very hard for those who have exercised great authority here in Church and State, and in the world of commerce and so on, to accept that their role is not *ipso facto* continued there. This is not an attack on those who have high office here whatever that office is. In any case, many of those who hold such office would feel they do so with responsibility and fulfil a necessary function here which they cannot expect to continue just by virtue of their position in this world. Those who think that they will inherit there, the privilege with which life has blessed them here are in for a rude shock. There are many great souls here, people of great faith and spiritual integrity, well down the list of worldly achievement who will be seen to be what they really are in the continuation of life. I meet them every day in my ministry and I have a great admiration for them. One man I think of, a truly Christian man, who looked after his dear wife following a very nasty stroke for many many long years, caring for her, taking her out in a pushchair mile after mile and on holiday and to church and to other functions, will I believe be truly seen to be what he is on the other side of life. Here, I do not suppose many would feel he was a great soul. But then we live in a world which pays a fortune to people to play snooker and organises mountains of surplus food which cannot be sent to millions who starve every year.

People often say to me, 'Do you ever have the experience of clergymen making their presence known from the other side of life?' They mean I suppose, do people who have been clergymen here ever make their presence known? The answer is 'Yes'. I have had several clergymen friends contact me briefly through

66

mediumistic people who never knew of them. A previous Bishop of this diocese made a brief contact one day, through a medium friend. Had the medium just said, 'There is a clergyman here whose name is Ronald.' I would not have accepted it, everyone knows of my association with him, that kind of thing is not evidence. But the words he conveyed to her after she had described him left no doubt in my mind as to his presence. On another occasion a former Assistant Bishop of this diocese was present and, through a medium friend, gave excellent evidence of his work in China of which she quite certainly had no knowledge. I also on one occasion had by name, assurance of the presence of the vicar of my parish church where I worshipped as a young man. The medium concerned did not even known the name of that church or its location.

Perhaps the most dramatic evidence of the presence of a cleric came some years ago when I visited London as a Proctor in Convocation (rather like an MP of the Church). There used to be an argument, I am told in past centuries, as to whether an Archdeacon could be saved. I am sure Archdeacons, and indeed all clergymen, have as much chance as anyone else. However, if they appear to the clairvoyant in some kind of ecclesiastical garb, it is for purposes of recognition only. I am aware that on the other side of life men who were Archbishops, Bishops and so on here do not there, go about dressed as they did on earth, anymore than footballers who have passed over go around in football shorts and shin pads. Those on the other side of life however, have the ability to show a picture of themselves in a form which can be recognised. I don't think we shall ever know how they do this until we get there ourselves. It has something to do with superior thought projection.

I was visiting London as a Proctor in Convocation for a meeting of the Church Assembly. I held this position for six years, the experience was very interesting. Much of the work was boring, but I suppose necessary, and in my time there we voted for, and created, the modern General Synod which is even more boring as far as I can judge. There were highlights of course. Very excellent speeches comparing more than favourably with the unintelligent shouting in the House of Commons and the over-polite chirping in the House of Lords. One of the great moments was, for instance, when Christopher Wansey would rise to oppose something the establishment so earnestly desired. He would begin by praising the excellence of form and delivery of some Archbishop or Bishop and then lament that it was sad that so much learning and talent had been lavished on such a travesty of fact that it compared ill with the debates of the third form in his schooldays. His wit was delightful and something out of *Yes Prime Minister.* These sallies helped to make the rest of the proceedings palatable, although try as one may it was hard going at times and I was never absent from the house I promise you.

In the evenings we were often free and being away from home we went to a theatre or to some musical concert. I remember one very funny evening when the Archdeacon of Loughborough and I finished a late session and, looking at our watches, decided that we could only make a theatre which was ten minutes away. Now ten minutes in London leaves practically no mileage. We arrived without the Archdeacon having being able to remove his clerical collar. I had with great foresight put an ordinary shirt and tie in my briefcase and had changed in the cloakroom in Church House. We had no time to look at the posters outside the theatre and had no idea what was on offer. It was the nearest theatre and in we rushed hopeful that we would have a pleasant surprise. Surprise we had sure enough. On the stage was a very large tank of water representing a swimming pool. A very attractive young actress in this play frequently took off all her clothes and swam nude in the tank. I am afraid Mrs Whitehouse would not have approved. I never allow myself to be thrown by anything in life but I do remember saying aloud, 'Crikey!' You must remember that such things were not as common as they are now. However, the real fun was in seeing the face of my Archdeacon friend, for he was wearing his clerical collar whereas I was not. His face became redder and redder and he sank lower and lower into his seat hoping nobody would notice him whilst I was convulsed with laughter, not at the so-called play but at him. 'After all,' I told him 'you are the father of three stalwart boys and such things must not be unknown to you.' He was not however inclined to heed such pleasantries, thinking only of his reputation. When it was all over he fairly sprinted from the theatre on to the other side of Whitehall fear-fully looking around to see if some passing Bishop or Archbishop was walking that way bound for his club, for they were all in London at the Assembly. He will not mind me telling you about this.

Such an experience was not to be repeated the next night and my friend had arranged to attend some sober meeting or other to which, as luck would have it, I was not invited. I was wondering what to do that night not being very anxious to return to my bed-sit although it was very comfortable. I had a telephone call from Margaret Wilson, a friend of Mrs Taylor, who was at that time Advertisement Editor of the *Psychic News*. She asked me if I was free that evening and I replied that I was and she said that she would pick me up after the Assembly. She would not say anything about our destination. She drove a Mini and after a fair drive we arrived at a well-known Town Hall. Attempts to get her to tell me what she was about failed. I just followed in her wake. We went up the steps and down a corridor to what was a back room or ante-room to a main hall.

Just before we entered this small room Margaret Wilson said to me, 'We are going to hear Jessie Nason.' Mrs Nason was a Jewish lady and a quite outstanding medium. I knew about her but I had never met her, Nella Taylor had often spoken about her. As we entered the room Mrs Nason said to me quite naturally, 'Oh here you are.' I shook her hand and thought that she was referring to the fact that Margaret Wilson had somehow told her that I was to be brought that evening. Apparently however, she had not told Mrs Nason I was coming or that she herself was attending her gathering that evening. I must say also that I had changed my clerical collar for a collar and tie and Margaret Wilson had intro-duced me as a friend of Nella Taylor from Leicester. She did not mention that I was a clergyman and afterwards I questioned Margaret about this because it had obvious importance in view of what happened. Mrs Nason then said, 'My guide tells me that you are to speak.' I was quite taken aback. I had no idea where I was going for the evening and had certainly not intended to speak anywhere. I am not backward in being able to get up and speak without preparation and that is well known but equally when I am going out to speak I do my homework carefully and am a great believer in doing so.

'Speak,' I said, 'heavens – speak about what? I haven't come to speak at all.' I laughed pleasantly enough although I felt somewhat at a disadvantage.

Mrs Nason was adamant. 'I am told that you will speak and I will give clairvoyance,' she said.

What could I do? I didn't want to get into one of those pantomime situations where I said, 'Oh no I won't,' and she said, 'Oh yes you will.' I had to pull myself together and so I replied, 'Very well I will talk for ten minutes on the use of the psychic in the ministry of an ordinary parish clergyman.'

We went into the main hall which was packed, not to hear me of course, they did not know I was coming. They were there to hear Jessie Nason. She explained that a friend was with her and would speak on his experience of the psychic as a tool in his ministry as a clergyman. I managed to be bright and put over what I had to say with clarity and humour and it seemed to go down well. I hoped it might make some of those present consider the whole subject of life after physical death and re-examine their own attitudes. Then Mrs Nason gave her clairvoyance. I have explained that mediums like all of us have their good days and bad days. Sometimes things go right and sometimes they go wrong. This was one of her good days. She was absolutely on the ball. She first of all looked at a chap on the front row and said to him, 'I know you think I am a fraud. You've only come tonight to please your friend.' The chap looked very embarrassed and went slightly red but it was obvious that she had hit the nail on the head. He admitted that she was right. 'I know,' she replied, 'because your brother is telling me and he was a porter in Covent Garden and I can see him with all his baskets on his head.' The man's jaw dropped and his face was a study as she then mentioned the presence of a number of people he knew, describing them and giving evidence which was obviously correct and which he acknowledged and of which she could not have known. Then she switched to a good-looking well-made-up girl a few rows back. 'Don't worry,' she said to her, 'I know you have been to the T.V. studio for a test today and you are wondering if you will get the part, you will. Just wait, they'll be in touch.' The girl's face and that of a lady sitting by her, an older replica of the girl, obviously her mother, was a study. 'Am I right?' asked Mrs Nason.

'Yes,' answered the girl and Mrs Nason then told her who was telling her the information. It was correct. So she went on around the hall. I do not think she got one 'No' all through the meeting. She was in tune, conditions were right. It was quite astonishing to hear it all, although I was by now used to such occasions. Sometimes of course those present come with the express purpose of resisting the medium and making him or her look a fool or look wrong. I have had several experiences of that but not of anyone doing that to me. I remember Mrs Taylor once going to a young woman in a meeting and making known to her a close relative who then had a quite sharp message for her. The message was not offensive in any way, nor did it let her down in front of people, but it was to urge her to abandon a certain line of activity and to change her ways for her own good. The woman was immediately 'anti' and difficult. She rejected the whole thing and the person who was giving the advice. Some mediums would have turned away. Not Mrs Taylor. 'Don't know her?' she said. 'Don't know her? Of course you do. I want to go to a churchyard in Derbyshire. I go up a hill and under a Lych Gate. I go up the main pathway to the church and then turn off to the left. There are three graves. The one on the left contains the coffin of your aunt among others. On the right there is another grave but in the centre there is the grave of the lady who is giving you this advice. The headstone reads . . .' and she read out the complete reading on the headstone. It was comical to see the face of the woman who then began to cry gently. The message got home. Much good was done for that woman that night and hopefully she took the advice.

I return to my evening in London. After the meeting Margaret said to Mrs Nason, 'What are you doing Jessie?' 'Nothing,' she replied. 'Going home for some supper.' Margaret then invited herself and me along also. We drove to Jessie's flat and then had supper. After supper Mrs Nason sat down and said, 'Let us see what our friends want to say to you Ken'. Now I must explain again that she was a Jewess and had no knowledge of the workings of the Church of England and nobody had told her why I was in London. She then told me that her guide was wishing to put me in touch with a temple. I could not understand this. She concentrated again. 'No,' she said, 'with a man called Temple. He tells me that he once presided over the great meeting from which you have come.' I was somewhat taken aback by this. Of course I knew that William Temple, the greatest Archbishop the Church of England has known in modern times, had once presided over the Church Assembly where I had been all day. I could not however understand why he had come to me, an undistinguished minor clergyman. Later however I did understand. Of all the people in that great debating hall in Church House probably I was the only one who believed such a thing possible and was in a position to be with someone who had the gift of being able to put us into contact with one another. Mrs Nason said, 'He tells me he will visit you from time to time but not be a regular helper like your guides and that he will verify this present meeting with you at a later date.' Then he was gone.

I had just come to a crossroads at that time with my work of spiritual healing, about which I will write later on in this book, and Margaret knew this. She asked Jessie if they had any words to say about the healing. Her reply was, 'When the pupil is ready the master will appear.' She then described to me a person who had been a doctor in Austria when he was on earth. Much later that man was seen with me and indeed has made himself known on many occasions since.

I did not think too much about Mrs Nason's message from William Temple. It is easy to say such things and I am a wary bird in these matter. However, about six months later I was still investigating mediumistic activity and had gone along to an open circle. A little woman arose when the meeting was thrown open for anyone to make a contribution and came and stood in front of me. I had never seen her before and I have never seen her since. I understood that she came from Coalville. She said to me, 'I have a man here named Temple and he tells me that some time ago he promised you that he would verify your first meeting.' 'That is quite true,' I replied. There was no more but what more could you ask for if you wished to be sure that it was possible to contact those who have passed on before you. He was spurring me on.

Giving a touch of encouragement to any thought of doubt which might arise when the problems I have mentioned above became evident.

The presence of another 'clergyman' was made known to me some years ago when I went to Leeds and co-operated in a great gathering of Christian spiritualists there. It was held in Leeds Town Hall, a fine and very pleasant Victorian building and it was packed. I spoke and Mrs Taylor gave clairvoyance. What she did was very accurate. She had a very clear way of knowing to whom she was to speak. She saw a small light which settled over the head of the person in that vast audience or, of course, in some smaller room. That was the person for whom the message from someone on the other side of life was intended. Later on at the home of Fred Moore who, with his wife, was doing wonderful work among unmarried pregnant girls and women who were in difficulties or rejected by their families, I spoke to the President of the Christian Spiritualist movement in London. He asked me if I ever saw a Bishop or Archbishop on the other side of life. I replied that I had occasionally done so and described the person. A very pleasant man with a very kindly but strong face dressed in full robes and mitre. 'Yes,' he said, 'that is the man. Do you know who he is?' I said that I did not know him and did not know who he was. He just appeared and smiled at me from time to time. He then told me that if I was to go to a certain well-known building in London I would find there an oil painting of the man. He knew his name but he just smiled and said, 'Why not find out for yourself?' My final comment on that is rather like one of those cryptic comments from Genesis 'And behold it was so.' Yes, clergymen return to make their presence known just like lesser mortals, or should it be greater mortals?

Perhaps I ought here to say that people must not be upset if their loved ones do not seem to return to them when they find themselves in the presence of a psychic person or mediumistic person. Those on the other side of life have their lives to live and those who understand the way forward will want to progress forward and into the sphere beyond the immediate sphere where they find themselves after life in this world. Love is the tie that binds and people who really love one another will not be separated in the long run, but we must allow those who precede us to live their lives and not to be standing at our elbow all the time. I often have some person made known to me by a medium friend whom I have known in my ministry and I am quite happy to renew that acquaintanceship. It would be all too easy to say, 'Why doesn't my mother come more often, or one of my dear friends or other loved relatives?' However I have come to realise that this is wrong and I do not expect them to be hovering around me all the time at my beck and call. I am grateful when they do come, but I am equally sure that I shall see again in due course all those I have loved and who love me. I have often had people visit me and very good evidence has been given of the presence of someone they knew who is now on the other side of life. They ask me, 'Why do you think my father or mother has not come?' I have to be honest and say, 'Frankly I do not know'. I am sure that the tie of love will never break if it is genuine and people must trust God until the great reunion takes place.

8

Not all Sweetness and Light!

It would be easy to pretend that all my experiences have been pleasant and to exaggerate or 'write up' the evidence so that people received an entirely false impression. Indeed some clergy abandon or dismiss any suggestion that mediumistic activity can be right and helpful because they have had an experience with a parishioner of the unhappy face of psychic activity – once bitten twice shy is their motto.

Not all my own experiences have been pleasant. I have said several times that the psychic activity which operates as a link with those on the other side of life is neither good nor bad. It can be used for either.

I recall a telephone call some years ago from the headmaster of a well-known school. He had a problem which concerned two of his senior girls. They had been operating a ouija board or a circle of letters in which there was a glass which moved when they put their fingers on it. This kind of thing very often leads to unfortunate situations. I am always warning people against doing it although many just regard it as 'a bit of fun' and do not take it seriously until something goes wrong. I lecture in a certain senior school and I find each year that there are a number of senior pupils who play with an ouija board situation. I always advise them to give it up. The two girls in question had made a contact with someone on the other side of life. This man had spelled out sentences to them and among the things he said were pieces of information which were correct. In fact he had also predicted certain things which turned out to be true. They had therefore come to take notice of him. After all if he knew those things he was likely to know much more and they had no reason to doubt that he did. The man was obviously a very low personality. Having trapped them into feeling that he was superior in knowledge to them he then told them that they would be killed one morning going to school. Now these girls went to school in a car. They were so frightened that they refused to go to school. The head had never had such a situation before. Office boys who take the day off to go to their grandmother's funeral are common enough until they seem to have had more than the permitted number of grandmothers but there cannot be too many cases of senior pupils staying away from school because those on the other side of life have told them they will be killed if they go. In some way the head had learned that I knew a fair amount about psychic things and persuaded the girls to see me. As they were not going to school in the morning, the venue and time which their contact had outlined as the situation of their transition to the next world, they came with a teacher to see me one afternoon. They were two very intelligent girls and very pleasant. I immediately picked up with one very strong latent psychic ability of which she was not aware. She was the 'power house' which had made this contact possible. I asked them who George was, they looked sheepish. George was the name they had given to the man they had contacted. I was told by my own guide that the information he had given them was mischievous and wicked and quite incorrect. He was just enjoying playing with them. A cat and mouse game. I put them in possession of some knowledge about the other side of life and about those on the first plane who were no different to when they left our earth, many of whom were no more to be trusted than they were here, anchored down unable to progress until they changed their ways. The girls said that all they wanted was to be free of George and his influence. I then prayed with them and asked God for His protection for them and that a barrier might be put around them through which this villain might not penetrate. I then spoke to him by thought in no uncertain way just as I would to anyone terrorising young people here. I am glad to say that that was the end of the matter. They did not again engage in this foolish excursion in psychic power into something unknown for which they were not equipped. A little time afterwards I met one of the girls who was a musician playing at a function I was conducting and she was bright and cheerful with that fear put behind her.

Sometime before that I had a phone call from a woman who was quite distraught and when she eventually visited me with her husband I could well understand why. It seems that one night she and certain friends had been 'doing' the ouija board just for fun. Her husband had declined to join them and was just sitting, watching, in an armchair. Suddenly, he seemed to be possessed and to utter strange noises which might have been a foreign language, then he stood up, picked up a large settee, normally beyond the strength and ability of one man to manhandle, and hurled it through a plate glass window. This woman, just an ordinary soul, although very frightened, put her hand on his head and prayed with all her might until he fell quiet. They were terrified in case this situation should recur. As I sat I saw a very old man sitting in the middle of a village somewhere out East. All around him was devastation. Troops had passed that way and they had not left one person alive in the village except him. He was very very old. Men, women and children lay all around him, dead. Huts were on fire. He just sat there dazed, moaning and wailing. I asked the man who had visited me with his wife, whom I had never seen before if he had ever been out East, in the forces. He said that he had. I described to him what I saw and he nodded. They had come upon several villages like that. I took his mind back to the old man and to what he had done for him. I felt that he had been kind to the old man in so far as was humanly possible. He nodded. This man had died in great shock. He had fastened himself on to this kindly soldier and after his physical death had continued to link closely with him and would not leave him. The group operating the ouija board contained several people with latent psychic energy which had built up and the old man had been able to make his presence felt in this violent way being still in a most disturbed state on the other side of life. We prayed for the old man, that he would be healed and helped by those there to whom so far he had not responded and the couple who had come to see me promised that they would never again indulge in psychic activity for which they were not trained. You may think it an unlikely story! I am simply recounting what happened. 'There are more things Horatio . . . .'

I have never wanted to be, nor will want to be, a seeker after

77

physical phenomena of a psychic kind but there is plenty of it about. There is not a city in the land which does not possess one or more dwelling houses in which very strange things take place. Objects are moved about, voices are heard, people are frightened. I do not like people to be frightened and so sometimes I am drawn in to help. I have no desire to be a 'ghost hunter'. I recall some-time ago receiving a telephone call from another vicar not far away from my own parish, he explained that he was ringing me because he was very perplexed. He had been asked to help an Asian family who were in great trouble but the whole matter was beyond him. Indian people often have a great respect for priests even though they may not be of their own religion and I should explain that Leicester is one of those places where our friends from India have settled particularly. This family had begun to experience very unsettling phenomena in the house. Voices, noises, furniture was moved about, and finally something that was very serious, a large gas fire was pulled away from the wall, not only the fire itself but the very heavy tile setting in which it was placed. Fortunately no serious damage had resulted but obviously gas pipes cannot be treated in that manner. When I arrived at the house with the vicar the family showed me a very large old-fashioned double wardrobe which two men could hardly move and which really needed dismantling to shift at all. Apparently it had been thrust across the room without anybody touching it. The whole family was in a very agitated state of mind.

I had taken a medium friend along with me but it just chanced that it was me who began to latch on to the cause. I saw a man ploughing behind bullocks and was shown a particular spot on the map of India. The rest that followed was rather like the story of Snow White in which someone had been slighted and taken their revenge. I felt that we were concerned about a wedding and that the man I saw ploughing, whom I felt was a relative of this family had been deliberately excluded from certain village wedding celebrations through a quarrel. This was some time ago of course and he had passed into the continuation of life. Because there was in that family a 'power house', someone with a great deal of latent psychic energy, he had begun to plague them in the way they had experienced. One young man who could speak good English had to translate what I was saying into their Indian dialect as some of the older family members had little English. As he spoke, they became very excited and nodded their heads, he explained to me that what I had described was absolutely accurate and the man was an old uncle who had cursed certain people for the slight that had been put upon him. The vicar, a very able man was slightly dazed by this and small wonder. There had been a day when I would have been more than slightly dazed myself. My medium friend was able to add some further bits of information to what I had picked up and then we prayed to God that the interference of this man might be stopped and that he would understand that the old quarrel had passed and all must be forgiven. We asked for protection for the family and especially for a girl from whom the psychic energy flowed so freely. I felt all would be well and as far as I know it never went any further. If it had done I am sure they would have come back to me, as I have known Indian people persist with me in such things as long as they were troubled.

A year or two ago I had a visit from someone who lived in a former parish of mine. They had a situation in their home, one I had never visited in my time there, although it had been visited by my Church Army Sister who would have disapproved of all things unusual and psychic. She was a marvellous soul and a tower of strength but if she encountered anything strange on her visit I am sure that she would have turned away in disapproval. The person who came to see me told me that they had a constant visitor in the house from the other side of life. This visitor could be heard and his voice was that of a boy. The did no harm but they found things moved, windows open, bedsheets ruffled and so on. The experience was not confined to one person in the house. On visiting the house I could see a boy of about thirteen or fourteen and I felt a sense of tragedy about him and that he had attached himself to this family because they were a very warm-hearted and close family. We then discovered that some years ago a boy of this age had hung himself in that house. It was a very sad case. It was obviously not a situation that called for stringent measures and some who had advised exorcism were talking complete nonsense. The family did in fact accept this person and were not at all frightened. We prayed there and then for help to be given him and the family

79

said that they would continue to accept him and continue to pray for him until he could move away with those who would befriend him and help him on the other side of life.

It must be appreciated of course that I am not at liberty to write about some of the most interesting cases I have experienced because the situations involve the personal lives and business of people who have sought my help. I have been careful therefore not to mention names and I am afraid that in some cases I cannot begin to describe situations for fear that those reading might suddenly be aware of whom I am writing. If a priest breaks confidentiality then he is no priest. My task is simply to get people thinking anew.

I have a friend who is a very fine medium and a good Christian man, to whom people come from great distances for help just as they did to Nella Taylor, (in her case they flew to see her from the continent and in the case of this gentleman people often make the journey from Ireland). He went into the bank recently to pay a bill and was somewhat alarmed when the bank clerk told him that the manager wished to see him. He naturally thought that his mathematics had broken down and that he was in the red. In fact the bank manager wished to have a sitting with him. This medium friend often had professional people to see him and in the past these have included high-ranking officials in government and the police and people who are very much in the public eye including actors and actresses and many very intelligent people who are seeking the truth about the continuation of life.

I once had a visit from a business man of some standing who lived in the county, and was experiencing some very disturbing situations in the lovely home he was renting for the time being. The interesting thing about this situation to me was not so much the peculiar nature of the experiences but that he had been to a Roman Catholic priest for help and found the priest very kind as one might expect. When the nature of the problem was revealed the priest had invoked the help of a colleague who had brought with him a nun who was psychic. She was mediumistic. Now the Roman Catholic Church has in my experience always been very critical of psychic things and tends to regard them as bad or at least to be left well alone. One might have thought that when it was discovered that this nun was a psychic she would have been told by her superiors to abandon her gift completely and been put under obedience to do so. In fact this had not happened and she had been put under the control, if I may put it like that, of a senior priest who was allowed to use her gift when he felt it was right. In this case they were not able to help the man much. I called in the help of a friend of mine who is very good with these cases of unusual phenomena from the other side of life and together we were able to unravel why these things were happening and able to advise the man of the line he ought to take to be free of the situation. More I must not say. As far as I know he took the advice and the problem passed.

One of the difficulties in dealing with situations where those on the other side of life impinge on people here is that it is hard often to get the person here, who is experiencing difficulty, to play their own part in throwing off the undesirable influence. You can tell people to say the Lord's Prayer and the Twenty-Third Psalm and so on as many clergy do, till the cows come home, but if they do not exert their own will in the matter the condition often returns. In some cases they readmit the situation by fear. It is rather like the rabbit and the stoat. The rabbit could easily distance itself from the stoat but it is fearfully mesmerised by it and that is its downfall. I have known so-called exorcists declare that they have 'cast out' a spirit and the forceful nature of the exorcist seems to have done the trick, but after a time the influence is back again because the person in difficulty has readmitted it. They then become despondent and do not go back to the exorcist who goes blandly on his way thinking all his geese are swans and that he is always successful.

It is just the same with clairvoyance. A medium will often be told that what she or he said to someone seeking help, has taken place. It is not so often that the person will go back to the mediumistic person and tell them that they were wrong. Nella Taylor always admitted that when I discussed these things with her. It behoves none of us to be arrogant or to feel we are always right whether we are mediumistic or not. There is a great reluctance in the spiritualist church to admit that mistakes occur. But, mistakes are part of life. To imagine that because a person has passed through the transition to the other side of life that they never make a mistake is, of course, nonsense. If we allow ourselves to feel that they are like God himself and always right, then we have only ourselves to blame. We must exercise common sense and not expect more than we should. That is why, to me, the most important thing about psychic communications is to establish the continuation of life. The knowledge that there is continuation of life after this period on earth is very important to us all. Taken seriously it ought to bring about a whole new approach to life generally although it may not remove difficulties entirely whilst we trudge along our earthly pathway. If those on the other side of life see some of the events on that pathway and are able to encourage us when they are reached, or if they can warn us of some coming disaster which can be avoided and by doing so not interfere with our free will in any way, then that to me is an added bonus. After all, when I have heard people objecting to mediumistic help, I have simply asked the objector, 'If you saw a person about to do something very dangerous or silly through lack of knowledge, would you point out the danger to them?' Why should those on the other side of life not do that if they do in fact see things going radically wrong. If I am asked why our friends on the other side of life do not warn us more often I can only make an assumption that they do not see everything before us and I do not know why they seem to see some things and not others.

We have talked about the influence of people from the next world who are of low principles, but there are many there who have high principles and are good people who would help prevent much of what happens to hurt people if it was in their power. That they do not do so obviously to me means that they cannot do so. I have heard a guide speaking through Mrs Taylor outline the most wonderful philosophy of life which if followed would make this world a quite different place but that advice is not followed. I seem to remember that another more important person spoke words of grace a very long time ago which also are not followed, although if they were we should all live in peace and share the resources of the world. His name is Jesus Christ.

9

Physician Heal Thyself

Long ago our Lord was aware that people were critical of him because they felt they knew him and were therefore unwilling to accept his words. The quotation at the head of this chapter comes from St Luke's fourth chapter where Jesus had gone into the synagogue on the sabbath and they had given him the roll of parchment on which was recorded the Scriptures from which to read. He read some very resounding words from the prophet Isaiah and then as he handed back the roll, he declared that on that very day the prophecy was being fulfilled in their sight. They were irritated with him. He told them that he was aware that they thought he should do there what they had heard he had done at Capernaum. Instead of showing them his quite astonishing powers he gave them some very sound and penetrating advice but whilst they might have easily been impressed by a miracle or a piece of precognition they didn't want a sermon and they were annoyed with him. In fact they took him and expelled him from the community. Let those take notice who think what wherever Jesus went he steamrollered people by his extraordinary and exceptional abilities. He used such powers sparingly. Indeed one could almost say he seemed to use such powers only where they were needed with particular people. The account of his temptations in the rough countryside our bibles call 'the wilderness' are interesting. First he was asked to assuage his hunger by making bread out of stones. I always think that this was deeper than a merely personal temptation to use his power for his own ends. Feed the world today and the world would be at his feet. Free food would give him unlimited power. He was tempted also to cast himself down from the temple in full view of a crowd who would quickly spread the news when the angels gently brought him to the ground. Fear of what he would do next would bring him such a following as had never hitherto been seen without force of arms. Then we are told the Evil One promised him that he should have all the kingdoms of the world in his hand if he would acknowledge him and make evil superior to goodness. Jesus as we know rejected these temptations. He never used his power for his own ends. Indeed I have always seen the treachery of Judas in a different light to that which some regard it. Judas knew of the power of Jesus. Unfortunately he didn't use that power as Judas would have liked. He longed to see Roman legions stricken to the ground in blindness. Might not the emperor himself come cap in hand to Jesus, for who could raise a man from physical death, give sight to the blind, heal leprosy and so on. Let Jesus show that he was invincible and the Jew would rule the earth. It was clear he was not going to do this, indeed he talked about going to die at Jerusalem. Judas was an intelligent man who kept the accounts, he was horrified. But, if he forced the hand of Jesus, Jesus would have to use his great powers in the way Judas wanted him to do. He went and told the enemies of Jesus where they could find him. But it all went wrong. Jesus did not do as Judas had felt he would. His victory was spiritual and with eternal consequences not merely an earthly battle.

Mediums are often regarded with awe and people who know mediums or attend churches which contain a number of local mediums often feel that those mediums know things about them without being asked for help. On the whole this is not true. Mediums who are genuine, find that it is quite enough to deal with the people who ask them for help without tuning in to every person they meet. It is also almost a universal fact that mediums do not get anything for themselves. 'Physician heal thyself' is I suppose often levelled at them. Nella Taylor who was such a help to people, proving the continuation of life, and so often being able to give them good advice from her guides, never received things for herself, nor much for her close friends and her family. I have found this also to be true of other mediumistic people.

I recall one excellent medium friend, Jack Corbett, who had done tremendous work, becoming unwell so that for quite a time he did not feel tuned in to those influences upon which he had been able to draw to serve other people. He, in fact, felt that his 'working days' in that respect were at an end. One of the most interesting things about his mediumship was that he had been able to go to Holland and France and conduct services and speak in Dutch and French – languages he did not know. When he ascended the platform to exercise his mediumistic gift, he allowed his guides to operate and was able to speak to his hearers fluently in their own language. If we go to the Acts of the Apostles, in chapter two we have there an account of what happened at the Feast of Pentecost at Jerusalem. Jerusalem was a cosmopolitan city because Jews from different nations made the journey there to visit the Temple. There were Parthians and Medes and Elamites, people from Mesopotamia, Judea and Cappadocia, Pontus and Asia, from Phrygia and Pamphylia, Egypt and Libya, also Cretes and Arabians and of course people from Rome. The apostles began to speak about Jesus in the languages of the different people who were gathered. Some have said what is recorded is an instance of the apostles speaking in tongues, a kind of ecstatic utterance which required a person with a special gift to understand the sounds they made. Paul refers to this phenomenon and says that he would rather speak five understandable words, than ten thousand words in a tongue which is not edifying. But, the account does not refer to 'tongues' it says that they all heard the message of the apostles in their own language. When you become aware of the way my medium friend was able to speak in Dutch and French without knowing those languages you begin to understand what happened at Pentecost. Now Jack, as I say, felt that his days of journeying around to exercise his gift were over. One day I was sitting with him in his home and I 'saw' a person who was known to him on the other side of life and I was told that he would in fact suddenly be called upon yet again to use his gift and travel in doing so although not as extensively as in the past. I could tell by the look on his face he really had some doubts about all that. However in due course one day a group of friends told him that they were taking him out with them and told him how to dress for the occasion and so on and that it was to be a surprise. He entered into the spirit of the thing and they went a motor journey of some miles and instead of entering a restaurant or some such establishment they came to a building which he knew was obviously housing a meeting of some kind. When they entered they told Jack that together with one or two others they had 'booked him' to take a meeting which was concerned with mediumistic guidance and help. Immediately he felt a qualm as he had decided that his active days in these things were over. When greetings had been exchanged and he found himself on the platform the situation became even more intense for him as the other speakers had not turned up. He ended up by speaking and using his gift as he had done so well for so many years. The point I am making is that he personally had no knowledge that this was to be. He did not receive the message about his renewed activities himself. In fact he did begin to travel afield again and has taken many meetings since.

Of course we would not want to know many things about our future, especially if we could not change them. Some things are best dealt with when they arrive. You can occasionally prepare for some tragedy or misfortune but often the resources of human beings especially allied to the Grace of God cope with the most crushing blows. One would only become ill and worn out with worry if some things were known a long time ahead. As with most things in life there has to be a balance. I have often visited a home and known that someone there who was ill was not going to recover, albeit having a wonderful life to look forward to ahead. One does not disclose such matters except in very exceptional circumstances. One builds up the person spiritually and supports those around who care. Mediumistic knowledge carries with it a great degree of responsibility. Often one has wished that one did not know some things but the back of a mediumistic person has to be very broad and has to bear many burdens if the gift is used correctly.

To return to the matter of mediums not picking up anything for themselves, I recall the visit to Leicester of a very famous medium who has since become more famous. I was impressed with his manner, his humility, the quality of his address and the standard of his clairvoyance. After the meeting my friend Nella Taylor said to me, 'I was watching you and you were "seeing" something were you not?' I admitted that I had seen something. I told her that I saw behind the medium on the platform the stern of a ship and he was standing at the stern waving goodbye. The ship was pointing out across the Atlantic. I must explain that if I ever see a ship or a plane pointing away it is usually coupled with a journey away from here; if it is pointing towards me it is usually coupled with a journey of someone to this country. If I see it sideways it is probably not a journey at all but is then expanded into a message in which ship or plane has had some past part to play. Standing on the quayside I saw a woman. She was dressed very colourfully and I was able to describe her in detail; her appearance and clothing and jewellery. I felt very strongly that this medium knew the woman and if he did not make that journey his whole work would suffer. Now the one thing mediums do not like is psychic persons in the audience coming up to them afterwards and saying, 'I saw one of your guides, as you were speaking.' I therefore had no intention of passing on what I saw. Mrs Taylor however seemed more than interested. 'Not only do I know the woman,' she said, 'but many of this medium's friends know her too. She has an overbearing influence on him which is not for his good and we are disturbed about it because he has such a great gift. I think you should tell him what you saw and were told.' I was not very keen. Finally I decided that I would approach him and he realised that he was being given really loving and sound advice from those who cared. Not long after, he left for North America where his work was acclaimed.

People ask me if I am ever told things for myself. The answer is almost always 'No'. For the most part I just sense a direction in which I feel I ought to go. I rarely pick up things for my own family. I did once receive a piece of information of great importance for a member of my family which if heeded might have made a great difference but it was not. People have to live their own lives. Members of my family however, who all live their own lives without mediumistic guidance are aware that help is often given to other people in this way. They have no hesitation however in asking for spiritual healing and I have promised to write about that at the end of this book. I am often asked if my medium friends have been able to give me communications from those on the other side of life which have been personally significant. The answer is, 'Sometimes but not often.' One friend who is a truly great medium has in fact been known to be irritated by the fact that he seems to get nothing with me at all. I am obviously not intended to be on the receiving end of mediumistic help. Somewhere, someone has decided that I must personally make my own way with God's help without being bolstered up with forecasts of things which will happen on my pathway. Mind you I have received great kindness from all my medium friends and much encouragement and that means a great deal. Those who have a true gift are not trapped into trying to give a senior canon a message as a proof of their own ability. They know that messages which are not genuine or messages which are slight and expanded by the so-called medium would only serve to put me off. I recall a woman who was a budding psychic once telling me of some future promotion. She said to me, 'Could you be an Archdeacon?' I knew she was fishing. I replied, 'Madam I could be Archbishop of Canterbury if I was asked.' It reminds me of the story of the medium who stood on the platform and said, 'I want to come to that lady on the front row. Hello dear! I am picking up red with you, lots of red. What colour is your car?'

'Green' came the reply.

'Ah, bear with me I am still there with the red – what colour is your house?'

'White,' came the reply.

'Ah white – I'm still with the red – what colour is your sitting room?'

'Pink,' came the reply.

'Ah, Pink sitting room, green car, white house – what colour are your husband's eyes?'

'Brown,' came the reply.

'Ah, I know where I am,' went on the medium. 'Have you posted a letter in the past month?' There is nothing more irritating or discrediting than people who claim to a psychic gift who 'fish'. I have often seen a 'medium' asking if anyone in the audience knows John. Of course scores of them do. Gradually by fishing she narrows on to someone who is bending over backwards to supply information unknowingly and in the end gives themselves a message.

Nella Taylor used to say at the beginning of her meeting, 'Do not give me any information. Just answer Yes or No.' I never knew her to ask any question of an audience which might be classed as 'fishing'.

I have a friend who has a very true gift and is more than helpful to everyone genuinely needing help who has ever approached her. Some years ago she found herself in a very unenviable situation. She had had a very difficult life, being one of those people who, try as they may, seem to run into one difficulty after another. In due course she met a very nice gentleman who wished to marry her. But it was not possible because of problems with his wife, who was something of a tartar and from whom he was separated. She was determined to cause him as much difficulty as possible right down to the bitter end and final letter of the law. At every turn things seemed bleak and they were faced with years of waiting. One day we were sitting having tea, when I was told that in fact the whole matter would be resolved suddenly, because the difficult lady would herself wish to be free to pursue other interests. In fact she would turn right about to facilitate her own new interests. My friends were very polite and listened to me but it was obvious that they felt that the likelihood of such a situation, in view of what they knew, was slender indeed. However it was so, and when things began to move they moved apace and in due course they were able to marry happily.

As I keep repeating, my main interest is to prove to people who are in doubt, the goodness of God in giving them the life ahead but sometimes the help given to people on their earthly journey is not without its value especially if it is given to someone who in their own turn has been such a help to so many but who cannot pick up things for themselves.

I mentioned earlier, the psychic gift is often with people from birth, but not always and some develop it much later in life. A friend of mine who has just retired from his work as a Deputy in the Coal Mines, and was a worshipping member of the Church of England, developed his psychic gift in middle age. Since that time he too has been a great help to a great many people, rather more than he could have been by acting as verger in his local church. Several times I have been able to describe to him people there with him who were members of his family, or friends from the past. I was able once to pass on to him an encouragement from friends on the other side of life. They told him of the work he would do ahead to help people and that he would retire at a certain time of the year twelve months ahead when such a thing was certainly not on the cards as far as he was aware. However it was so. He has since gone on from strength to strength and been a blessing to many people always voicing his devotion to Jesus Christ. Mediums do not generally receive things for themselves.

I remember once telling Nella Taylor that I saw a ship with her pointing away from this country towards North America and that she would go there fairly soon. She gave me a very hard look and I suppose could have been forgiven for thinking that I was in this instance well wide of the truth. She had no plans for going to North America. In fact within days she had a request to go to Canada, with her expenses paid, she had a remarkable tour and made a great impression. I am always of the opinion that medium-istic abilities just do not work on television and radio when it becomes almost a kind of media game with interviewers setting the usual questions, and often personal prejudices are so evident. So often the people being interviewed are terribly naive and seem unaware of the traps being laid before them. They are made to look quite silly. I once saw a very good medium with whom I once had a passing association – Albert Best, give a very sound inter-view on television. Most interviewers seem unable to remain unbiased and are unable, through lack of knowledge, to know how to go about securing the real truth – which includes knowing the kind of medium to approach. After all anyone can find so-called mediums who are full of imagination and self-deception. Mrs Taylor went to Canada as I have said, where she did a phone-in programme on the radio and was able to help many people through linking in to their voice pattern. There are few however, who can avoid intimidation and manipulation at the hands of experienced television interviewers.

In saying that I have not received much in the way of personal guidance about the future through my medium friends, I would not want any of them to feel I am ungrateful for all they have said to me by reason of encouragement. People often think that it must be quite difficult for me as a Canon of the Church to admit to being psychic, and that I must get opposition. In fact I have had very little. People know me for whom I am. They know me for my love of sport and for my sense of humour. They are aware of my very down-to-earth stance on every issue of life and they are aware of my devotion to Our Lord and His Church and the soundness of what I teach and preach. If I have used psychic ability, where it is appropriate to help people sometimes, it is never intruded and the truth is that people who have known me for years are astonished to know of this interest and means of guidance. These things are a part not the whole. In fact, through my medium friends I have received excellent evidence personally of loved ones on the other side of life. If little has been said to me about the future, then in my case, that is as it must be.

I have several times been given excellent evidence of the presence of my mother and father, grandparents and uncles. I once had excellent evidence of the presence of my brother's wife who had died when quite young. I only wish that evidence had been given to him and not to me. When I came to Belgrave the church treasurer was a woman of remarkable Christian character called Bessie Orton. Her goodness and kindness were known and appreciated by the whole congregation. She taught in the Sunday School, worked in the Sewing Party, polished the church woodwork and in fact did so much it was quite astonishing. If ever there was a pillar of the church it was Bessie Orton. She had been a director's confidential secretary in her day and carried that able administration into her local church. 'Don't forget Vicar, you have to go here, or there! Don't forget on Tuesday you need to sign this or that! Looking ahead don't you think we should decide about these functions?' She never allowed me to forget anything and I was able to leave much in her very capable hands. Even the Managing Director of I.C.I. was not better served in administration. Bessie had nursed her parents, her aunt and also her brother through terminal illness. Her faith was bright, her quiet influence sure. If you wanted to answer the question, 'What is Christian?' you could well have answered 'Bessie Orton'. Then she herself had a stroke. This was a severe blow not only to her but to all of us, this kind, sweet person, stricken down unable to speak properly. I had watched my father die of cancer and my mother and now this great friend. These experiences have always made me very sensitive to people in their troubles. For a long time doctors and their staff tried to improve Bessie's sad affliction but to no avail, she had another stroke and died. It was a grievous blow to the local church. Then a little time afterwards I was sitting visiting an elderly lady who is a psychic but who lives a long way from his area and, being a spiritualist, is not a member of my church. She said to me, 'There is a lady standing next to you who used to sew and care for the church, she is opening some books and adding up columns and her name is Bessie Horton.' I was so delighted. This woman had absolutely no knowledge of Bessie or of her work at St Peter's where she had been treasurer. 'Not Bessie Horton,' I said, 'Bessie Orton.' The very slight error made the evidence even more credible. I said to my friend, 'I wish to ask a question.' She nodded, 'How does she find things where she is?' The answer was prompt. 'She says that she is very happy but it is different from what she thought it might be.' I am sure it was and is. Many people are going to have something of a shock. Let none of us think that we are going to carry over with us either status or privilege. None must think they will carry their material prosperity with them.

The interesting thing is that this very nice person who was able to link up with Bessie Orton, one day had from me several pieces of evidence of the presence of people on the other side of life. I can remember giving her evidence about her aunt, with whom she had lived, and several people from her early days. I suppose the most dramatic instance was when I saw a man who was leading a fox on a lead. I told her what I was seeing, namely a man with a fox which was a pet. She knew him immediately. Then I saw the same man in a bus driver's uniform. She nodded. When she was young, long before she met her present husband she had this friend who had a fox as a pet and he had, in due course, become a bus driver. He had wanted to marry her but her aunt, in the days when guardians exercised real power, had considered that he was not good enough for her and intervened and sent the young man packing. That was a very long time ago and they lost touch. He had obviously passed onwards and now came back to her to make his presence known. I am always better pleased when contact of this nature is made rather than being told of some future prediction.

As I was writing this chapter I had to break off to visit a charming man in my parish, no longer young, who has been separated from his wife for the time being by her sudden death. He was devastated. On visiting the house I met his family who came from Wales. They are a close family and extremely nice people. They reminded me that I had buried a relative of theirs some years before and they had not forgotten what I said to them on that occasion. Thus encouraged I comforted them further, saying that I was certain that they would see the lady again, wife, mother, sister as she was. I could see a woman standing by the bereaved gentleman. She was not his wife and of a different generation to himself. I mentioned this and described her in particular the chain she wore around her neck which had a kind of medallion, a brooch-like affair on the end of it. The man knew her immediately and had a photograph of her wearing this chain and medallion which she often did. It was his mother. She said that the gentleman's wife was fine and was with her and all was going to be well with her. I always point out to people who understand and who respond to what I say, that I am sure that when those on the other side of life draw close to us and pick up our thoughts, as I know they do, and find that we are grieving as people without knowledge, as if they have gone forever, it must be very sad for them. However, if they see us acting, as people with understanding, knowing what has happened to them, they are much better able to get on with their lives on the other side until the reunion takes place.

10

The Little Things Matter

Often it is the little things that matter. Small things that the mediumistic person cannot possibly know about. I remember once burying a gentleman who was a member of the fairground fraternity. They are a very close fellowship and know one another all over the country. When there is a wedding or a baptism they come in large numbers. Funerals are especially well attended as they come to pay their last respects. Some of them wintered in one or two places in my parish. I had never met the gentleman who had died. Naturally after being asked to take the burial service I visited the family as I always do. They were living in a very handsome caravan. The walls were covered with Crown Derby and other objets d'art. The interior of the caravan was a revelation. The lady whose husband had died was, naturally enough, very unhappy and depressed. Her main concern was to know if he had continuation of life. I spoke to her gently and, I hoped, reassuringly. Then the burial service took place. A few weeks afterwards her son rang me to say that they were actually part of a fair in the parish at that moment, but that his mother was terribly depressed and that he was very worried. She had listened to me but could not be convinced that her husband still lived on. I went down to the fairground and found the caravan and the lady and sat with her to try and comfort her and resolve her doubts. As I did so I saw a sweeping sand-rimmed bay and was told it was Rhyl in North Wales. I asked her if she had ever been to Rhyl. She said, 'No,' they always worked the east coast – Skegness and along that coastline. I had to persist and said, 'I feel sure that you have been to Rhyl.'

'Oh well once,' she said. 'My husband and I went there for one day a very long time ago.'

'And you walked right around the sands,' I said.

'Yes,' she replied.

'How could I know that?' I asked.

'You could not know about it,' she said. 'I had almost forgotten myself. It is the only time I have ever been in Rhyl.' Then she realised that I could not know unless I was being told. Her husband then showed me his hand. Part of a finger was missing. I told her about this.

'Yes,' she said, 'he got his finger trapped in a piece of fairground machinery and it took the top from his finger.' Then he showed me his ring finger and it had on it the widest wedding ring I have ever seen.

'Yes,' she said, 'he had a piece of gold melted down and made into this wedding ring and it was really too big but he wore it.' She was convinced. She was not a happy soul because she was missing her husband but she knew I could not have guessed with such accuracy and accepted that someone was telling me what I passed on to her.

Very often things are communicated from friends on the other side of life just to reassure us of their presence. After all not every conversation we have with one another here is of epoch-making significance. I sometimes feel that people who are looking to criticise, whilst occasionally justified by the triviality of what is said, expect too much. They surely don't expect friends or family to be uttering words of vital importance on all the major issues of life, at every turn of the road. I recall once being in the house of a friend of mine, Ken, who had served in the Royal Navy. Suddenly I was being asked from the other side of life to mention to him quite the most extraordinary piece of information which seemed to me to be sheer nonsense. The picture was shown to me of a man in naval uniform and I saw him standing beside a very small submarine, a very tiny ship indeed. Then I was shown the fjords of Norway and I felt that this man had in fact taken part in an attack by midget submarines on a battleship which had sought refuge in a fjord. I recalled vaguely some newspaper story about the incident but what had this to do with my friend? Then, I felt that Ken had had something to do with this man but that the relationship was not close. Ken had served in the Navy in the Korean War. He had not served in the 1939–1945 war. He had however come to know this naval officer who had taken part in a memorable attack on the Tirpitz in a Norwegian fjord. I saw, incidentally, a well-known newspaper, headlining the incident. I am aware that this could have been my own memory at work, but I was at a loss to know what it all had to do with Ken. Then I saw the same man standing on the deck of an aircraft carrier and he had something to do with directing the warplanes. I felt somewhat foolish. How could this officer who had taken part in that courageous attack in Norway in a midget submarine, be directing fighters on and off an aircraft carrier? I felt that it was most unlikely and the likely thing was that I was beginning to 'flip my lid'. In any case what had it to do with Ken who had not served in that war? I gave what I saw and expected him to shake his head and say, 'Sorry I don't know what you are talking about.' He didn't. In fact he was quite excited. As I have mentioned above, he knew the man – not when he piloted the midget submarine, nor when later he transferred to the aircraft carrier to be in control of aircraft 'Commander Air' – but later on when Ken joined the Navy. He did however, know about the incidents I was being told about from the other side of life. I had thought the information didn't ring true, but it did. It was being given by an old naval friend, now on the other side of life, to prove his life there and presence with us. He knew about Ken serving under this officer and used it as evidence. On 30th December 1994 a newspaper carried a long obituary about the naval officer in the message who had risen to high rank and had passed onwards. As I have said, Ken had served under him in the Far East. You may say, 'So what – it didn't contribute anything to life.' It was not meant to. It was meant simply to prove the presence of someone on the other side of life who knew of my friend's past association which was unknown to me and offered it as proof of his own presence.

I am aware that the best proof is when a communication outlines something that is unknown to both sitter and clairvoyant which then has to be investigated and proved correct. But – life is a mixture. We have that kind of proof sometimes, but I can assure you that I am not able to latch into a person's past and lift information as accurately as in the case outlined above. My friend told me that he had not thought of that man for years and years. I now have great experience of people in a long ministry, and I am aware that certain people who are very close have a kind of understanding which is almost telepathic, but I defy anyone anywhere to pick up information such as I have outlined above, which was so dramatic and unusual, as accurately and as swiftly as it occurred. Ken who is a fine spiritual healer was approached in this way for reasons thought to be very sound by those on the other side of life.

Some time ago I was being driven to a funeral by a very pleasant young man employed by a well-known and respected firm of undertakers. This young man said to me that he had been listening to what I said at funerals, it greatly interested him and he wished to speak to me about it. He told me that he had listened to what I said with great interest because he felt around him the presence of someone who was unseen, but he felt it to be a good influence. I was able to tell him that the presence he felt was of a man who was a relative, but going back several generations. I described him in the uniform of the armed forces, pill-box hat and so on of the turn of the century. I wanted to be back in the days of the relief of Mafeking and the South African war. He did not recognise the man. However the picture was so strong and the influence so clear that I asked him to go home and tell his mother of what I said and see if she could help. I felt that she would do so. Some time later he was driving me again and he told me that he had done what I suggested and that his mother had given him a very old-fashioned look and said little, but she had visited a relative and returned with an old photograph of this man. I had in fact told him that there was a photograph of this man in his family. It was clearly the man I had seen and was a great uncle who had served in the forces and in those situations of which I had been told. The great uncle was very interested in this young man and was doing all that was open for him to do to help him along his pathway through life. He gave his surname, which was different from that of the young man and correct. The young man had a personal problem – don't we all? – and I told him of the line to take and the outcome in due course. Later it transpired that this advice was sound. The same young man decided to purchase a terraced house and was looking at a number of houses of this type. I described a house to him which

97

though far from new in every respect had a completely new sink unit. One of these houses had such a sink unit and after making an offer for it, he then discovered that a very long time ago his grandfather had lived in the same house. This would not alter the course of the world, but it is very interesting.

Not all the advice given by our friends on the other side of life is heeded. People have free will and they go their own way. I have referred to a member of my own family who was given right advice but who choose to go along another path and found the advice given had been correct. A very dear friend of mine, as so often in life, was ploughing a furrow concerning which he would brook no interference at all. It was doomed and bound to end in trouble and so it did. One very severe winter I warned him and his mother about repeated unnecessary journeys because I could see a very nasty car accident. Sure enough it took place and the car was a write-off. We were all glad that he escaped unscathed.

I recall a young man coming to see me who spent about half an hour doing what I would call 'twittering about' but in more sober language would be described as skirting the main issues which were really his problem. There was a lady with him on the other side of life who then told me the problem and after listening politely and patiently I cut across him and said, 'Do you know this woman?' I described her and gave some evidence of a very factual kind which established clearly who she was if he did indeed know her. He said, 'Yes certainly,' and he told me who she was. I then outlined his real problem as she described it to me – his jaw dropped. I then told him the advice given which would, with an effort, clear the way forward. He didn't like the advice and went away with mixed feelings being astounded as to how I knew about the problem without him telling me (although I described how I knew) but not wishing to accept the solution along the lines which were advised. I knew this is what would happen and that at some time ahead he would be saying, 'I wish I had taken the advice the canon passed on to me.'

Nella Taylor was very attached to her family and she regarded me almost as a member of it, as she did a dear friend whom she had known for many years. This friend had had a very difficult life. She had had a very unfortunate marriage and then a very happy one. Unfortunately this second marriage had not lasted long as her husband had died after only a very short married life. One day we were sitting in her pleasant home out in the country, when I was told to tell her that, in due course, she was going to meet a gentleman who would ask her to marry him. Her life would take on again a new meaning whereas at the moment she felt it had gone so wrong that sometimes she was very despondent. I described the gentleman. After a year or so she did in fact meet this gentleman, they were eventually married and are very happy. The information was given to me by her husband who had died, and he was obviously very anxious for her to have the companionship and help which he had not been able to give her by his early passing.

Not all our communications from our friends on the other side of life may have the same value but they are often important to the person concerned. Years ago a friend of mine who has been an outstanding medium and who had been brought up as a Roman Catholic, was taking a service in Leicester when he was asked to speak to a woman who had great difficulties in life because of a severe physical handicap. It always sticks in my mind because he came down from the platform to speak to this lady. He approached this lady and told her that in due course she would acquire a special vehicle and be able to get around and use the gift she had to help others. The lady concerned was feeling the problems of her handicap and was far from well and probably thought it most unlikely. However, he was right. She managed in time to master driving a Solo handicapped person's vehicle and did in fact go about using her psychic gift to help other people. I was having a cup of tea with her one day. (I know everyone thinks that parsons do nothing else but drink tea!) I saw her with a Mini and I told her that she would exchange her handicapped person's vehicle for a Mini and be able to have a passenger in this car which was not possible at the moment. I also saw the colour of the car which seemed to me to be a pale yellowy colour. Again she did not think this very likely. However in due course with encouragement she launched out and took driving lessons in a Mini and was able, after passing her test, to acquire one. Concerning the test she nearly abandoned the project because every time she took it something went wrong. Each time she did everything correctly except one thing. Next time she did that correctly and something else wrong. Many have had that experience. All I could say was, 'Keep going, because I see that car and I *know* you will drive it.' Eventually she passed the test. Before she obtained the car I thought a detail had gone wrong. She was and is a very independent person and had asked the car dealer for a red Mini because she liked red. I had seen a quite different colour and I was surprised, wondering why I had seen that colour and not the red she was insisting upon. However the dealer rang her to say that if she wanted a red Mini she would have to wait for quite a time, whereas he had in stock a car on which he could begin adaptions to cater for her handicap immediately. She wished to obtain the car quickly and agreed to have the one he had in stock which was in the colour range I had seen. Someone on the other side of life had certainly been able to see ahead accurately. You may say that all that was unnecessary. These things would have happened without the message having been given. No doubt that is true but the whole matter served to encourage her along her own pathway and to continue to use her psychic gift to help others. Mediums are not God or even Archangels. They need help and encouragement like us all. It is well known that I am very critical of the trivial nature of things given in meetings and services and I feel this does the cause of truth no good. People say, 'Fancy making a contact from the other side of life and using it for such a pointless observation.' I remember once sitting in a service in which an able medium eventually gave clairvoyance and dispensed messages all around the room. They were about objects which people present had on their mantleshelves and of which of course the medium could not have known. I am not saying she was wrong at all. She described one lady's cat which was at home, a home she had never entered, and so on. There were one or two people in that room known to me who were in desperate trouble and difficulty and who badly needed some help and encouragement but they did not get it. I went away very disgruntled. Somehow on the other side of life there was a bad slip-up. It was not that what was given was wrong, but it did not reflect a true sense of responsibility. I know sometimes people need only some small thing passed on from a loved one which causes them to begin to think deeply, but on the whole I do not wish to know about things in my past of which I am more than aware or to be told what I have on the mantleshelf even if I know that the medium has never been in my house. I would rather see a word of encouragement to some struggling soul or some spiritually uplifting message to bring light into the quest of a person who is seeking the truth. The guides of all mediums do not all operate on the same high standard. Again we are dealing with life. We are not all on the same level of understanding here or of the same agreed opinion on how life should flow or our own conduct operate. We are dealing with *people* on the other side of life not Saint Michael and his angels. At its lowest, clairvoyance can be a kind of game. A very valued friend of mine was once a very competent platform medium (as they are known when they can stand before an audience and give clairvoyance messages to a hall full of people). She more or less abandoned that for a real interest in healing and in spiritual knowledge which would advance the soul. In these departments she made considerable progress and arrived at a situation where she could teach others to achieve the knowledge she had, in a clear and yet uncompromising way. Her church was seeking a new president. One or two enlightened people knew that they had a wonderful opportunity to appoint her. They knew also that if they did she would give quite a new slant to the whole approach within that church. Spiritual progress would be at the top of the list and trivial clairvoyant messages well down. Unfortunately some, a majority, were not prepared to launch out on a really spiritual adventure, guided by her great experience. They preferred the little game of being told what they already knew, of uncritical acceptance of questionable messages, and they did not ask her to take the post. It has been their great loss. Clairvoyance and clairaudience are tools to be used at times, sometimes dramatically, but they are by no means the heart of or the whole of religion.

101

11

Evidence From Number 10

Now I know this sounds as if I am going to reveal astonishing and hitherto unknown events which have taken place in Number 10 Downing Street between cabinet meetings. I am afraid not. That kind of information would be worth a fortune in terms of payments from *The Sun* or *The News of the World*.

This Number 10 is a modest council house in Leicester tenanted by the friend I have mentioned already who assisted me for sixteen years with the spiritual healing in my church. Over the years Ken and I have sat and talked quite naturally over coffee in the presence of his wife who suffers from MS She sees clairvoyantly very occasionally and sometimes hears clairaudiently. My friend 'sees' on even less occasions. We have found however, that the threefold combination produces very often the right atmosphere in which we have received very interesting proof of the continuation of life. Mediums have their own way of putting this; they would say that he and his wife are 'power houses'. All I can say is that the evidence has been sometimes quite astonishing. Nothing could be more convincing than the evidence given of Ken's association with Commander Place which took place on a troop ship coming home from Japan when Ken took his kit aboard ship. I was told about the Commander's exploits against the Tirpitz in a midget submarine and of how he had then become the officer in charge of aircraft activity on an aircraft carrier – HMS *Ocean* in Korea.

On another occasion I was able to describe to Ken, a man in naval uniform and discourse on his favourite drink and several of his idiosyncrasies. Ken countered by asking for the number of gold bands on his epaulettes and this was given correctly. I was then told to tell him that he was nicknamed by the men 'Captain Bligh'. The officer was his Commanding Officer and commander of the flotilla and a very fine and able seaman of outstanding ability. On another occasion this officer was shown to me in a submarine, although when Ken had served under him it had been in mine-sweepers. This information also was correct as the man had been a submarine commander of first-class ability. One day I saw the picture given as evidence of his submarine being responsible for the sinking of another submarine. Ken told me that this was true. This was an unusual occurrence but Commander Bone, as he became had been in command of this exploit.

We had remarkable evidence given by those on the other side of life who had known Ken in his serving days. One piece of evidence was again graphically accurate as I recall it. I saw a man in naval uniform whom Ken recognised, and again he insisted on me giving him the man's insignia on his shoulders with the correct colour between the gold bands. This was because he was a Surgeon Commander. This colour was given correctly although I had no knowledge then of these things. I was told that the man had unfortunately been involved in a tragic end and I saw a shotgun. He had apparently died in a shooting accident, in which it was thought his dog sadly caused the accident with the gun. I also saw the operating theatre in which they worked and a picture of this man who was very explosive in character. Many great surgeons have been ice cold with the scalpel but quite caustic with their staff. I saw him hurl a scalpel at the door and it had in fact stuck in the door. This had happened in fact on an occasion when Ken was on duty as a naval medical theatre operative during an operation. Something had annoyed the surgeon and that was his response. For all that he was a fine surgeon and many had cause to be glad of his skill.

I always ask my guides to ask people who are trying to convince people with me about their continued life to give me some piece of evidence of which I have no knowledge at all, like the incident above. After all if there is some suspicion that the medium knows of the incident it can hardly be said to be good evidence. Sometimes I have been aware of the presence of someone but have been unwilling to just say, 'this or that person is here' without any evidence. Anybody can say things like that. I just rigidly dig in and refuse to go further. On the whole the guides are efficient and they help the person on the other side to select something which is known to the person to whom I am talking, but not to myself. On one occasion when the three of us were chatting away (we do not hold a seance or anything like that, if people link in they do, it is up to them, it is all very natural) Ken's wife's brother stood there and told me who he was. I was not prepared just to say, 'Your brother is here Gene.' After all such a statement without proof is useless. He showed me however, a naval MTB, a motor torpedo boat. When I told Gene I found it to be correct although Ken had never told me about his naval service. On another occasion an uncle of Gene's was present and he showed me himself in running kit, slightly old fashioned. This was also correct, her uncle Jim had won many cups in the army for running. If you ask me how they 'show' these pictures, I just do not know. It has something to do with thought projection on a level which is beyond us in our present state. Some here have the ability to screen the projected picture but the operation of it comes from the other side of life.

Gene's grandmother on wishing just to make her presence known to her showed me once a cowbell which she had by her bedside, and which she rang when she needed attention during the time she was ill on earth. She also spoke about a horse farm in Keswick where she was born. It is quite natural for our loved ones to wish to come near to us if they really love us. I have never been able to understand why come clergy insist that once you have laid aside the physical body, you must not have any further relationship with those whom you love and who love you. What nonsense! If your grandmother was kind and loving to you and one day, you went to the door and there she stood, you would say, 'How nice, come in Gran!' According to the attitude of those who seem fearful of those on the other side of life, we ought to say, 'Oh no Gran go away, you are dead, it is forbidden.' What rubbish. All the members of my family who have passed onwards were very kind and loving to me when I was young and if any of them wish to come near to me and bring the same kindness and love, they are more than welcome.

Ken's grandmother, not to be outdone, over a long period made several visits to us. On one occasion early on, because the guide would tell her that I was not prepared just to say this or that relative is here, she showed me a small shop and a shed in which ice-cream was being made. Years ago they had such a shop, long before my time in Leicester, in the Catherine Street area and indeed, made ice cream in such a shed. An aunt of Gene came one day and she showed me a cottage and a back room where she was making bread to sell from her cottage. This again was correct and Gene's Aunt Helen in this way gave evidence of her presence. She used to live in Cosby. Another uncle, Jack, gave proof of his presence on one occasion by showing me a dog which of course I described and he gave the name of the dog which was correct. Many of the things offered to confirm the presence of people were small things but very accurate. We have always been very careful never to fit anything to anything. Sometimes the evidence has been amusing. Sometimes not so, as when Gene's grandfather showed a farm building and I was told it was a building from which he fell tragically.

No evidence we have been offered over the years has been given in such volume or more correctly than by Ken's mother Violet. She herself on earth was aware of the ability of those on the other side of life to use the psychic ability of mediumistic people to link in with them. When Ken, years ago, was very unsure about the continuation of life and certainly of the possibility of linking with anyone who had passed on from this earth, his mother said to him, 'I will show you my lad when I get over there.' She has certainly done that and he acknowledges it. She has preceded anything she has wished to say to him or to Gene with a positive wave of things known only to him or to Gene and not to me. Again I would never say, 'Your mother is here.' That is a silly thing to say to anyone without giving evidence. This she has readily accepted and has shown absolute ingenuity in finding something however small, on every occasion, different from anything shown previously and all unknown to me. How long she can go on doing this I don't know. We just laugh at her resourcefulness. One of the most amusing items she showed me was a pair of ladies' unmentionables but they had the Union Jack on the seat.

Gene, Ken and I have known one another for such a long time that this was not as embarrassing a thing as it sounds. When I mentioned what she was holding up, they roared with laughter. Violet was a real character and despite a tough life, full of fun. She wore the knickers apparently to celebrate the end of the war and victory. Many expressed their relief in sillier ways than that. On one occasion I was shown a picture of her in overalls with a bib top. I must explain that sometimes I feel very diffident in saying what I see, because it seems all wrong and nobody wants to be thought a fool. I saw a lathe and metal shavings peeling from it. I waited for Ken to tell me he did not know what it was about but again his dear mother was not in the business of giving unrecognised evidence. She had apparently, in the war, worked in a small engineering concern like many women. On numerous occasions she would show some trinket or ornament which she had possessed and which they now possess and they would go and bring it out to prove the point. One such ornament was a pisces sign which wound on a little spindle in brooch form. Always she had some sensible down-to-earth piece of advice to offer and sometimes would show that she could see ahead where we could not. She assured us one day of army promotion for Ken's eldest son and in due course there it was just as she had forecast. One of the children, grown up and finding it hard to get a job, like so many, she said would secure a job within a very short time. That is always a very tricky prediction today – if you know anything about trying to find work. She was absolutely right and it happened only a few days afterwards. A year or two ago, Ken and Gene badly needed a holiday but it did not seem to be possible although his mother insisted that it would be so and insisted that it would be at the seaside. One of their sons in due course was moved to a post near the sea and, at the end of July, took his mother and father down for the holiday which seemed at one time to be remote.

Many of the things Violet has said to them of course are private matters, family matters and so on. In this book I have avoided any accounts connected with any people who have had good psychic evidence from me of the continuation of life which have been linked with very personal situations. A good medium like a good priest will not let down those who come for help. A medium who chatters about the very personal problems of people desperate for help is not worth the name.

Some things are quite light-hearted. Those on the other side of life are not always dealing with broken marriages and severe illness and so on. One day I went into Ken's house where I have always been received with great hospitality and a cup of coffee was in my hand before I could take off my anorak. As I sat down, his mother was there immediately with some small piece of evidence for recognition and then the picture of a large apple pie. I was a bit mystified by this and asked Ken what it meant. Suddenly he leapt up and rushed out of the room to the kitchen. On return he explained that he had put a large apple pie in the oven and had forgotten about it. Fortunately it was rescued in time – a trivial incident but interesting. Now I know that you can ask why more disasters are not averted and so on. I have not the answer to all that. In one way I am dying to get on the other side of life to see why this and why that and discover the answer to many questions I ponder all the time. Our friends there may not interfere with our free will although wicked forces try to do so and that accounts for some of the situations which perplex us. Other things are merely to show their awareness of what is going on around us. Often we are not in a receptive mood and this applies even to mediumistic people. Some things I suspect are beyond them for reasons we do not understand. All I know is that on the other side of life from those we have loved and still love and from those who serve God by trying to help those of us who live on this earth, there is a great wave of love and a great desire to help. If they could help, if it is permitted, if it is possible and in the great plan behind God's Eternal Purpose, they would do so. Of that I am sure.

Ken's healing ministry at Belgrave came to an end in due course and we were all most sorry to see him leave. We had had warning of this when one day I was having coffee with him and his wife. Violet made her presence known with one of those small but very accurate bits of evidence that were her trade mark. She then showed me a seaside coast line, not a deep bay but rather a curve in the coast and I could see Ken, wearing a top coat, pushing Gene in her wheelchair. It certainly was not summer, more

107

like November. We couldn't place this at all. Then within a few days his son, planning for his eventual retirement from the army decided to buy a property in Mablethorpe and suggested to his mother and father that they should go and live in it before (and after) he retired. It was obviously a good thing for them and they went at the back end of the year. You might say, 'Oh well they would have gone anyway.' That is true but we are just simply trying to establish that there is definitely continuation of life for all people, and that information should change our attitudes about the whole of life. I am saying that my experiences point to the fact that those who have laid aside their lives in this world are certainly continuing them on the other side like Ken's mother Violet.

I have mentioned earlier the blind medium and my extraordinary encounter with him at a well-known bowling club. After an illness of thirteen years he eventually died, leaving his wife Maud who is totally blind. In the emotional wake of such a parting there are always so-called psychics who immediately 'pick up' the person who has moved on. Fortunately Maud knows enough about it all not to accept everything uncritically. It seemed a long time before I was even aware of Michael's presence when I visited Maud but I have found it wise just to relax and let the contact come from them. If those on the other side of life come, they come. If they don't, they don't. I was visiting Maud one day, when I suddenly became aware that Michael was there. He showed me a folding ruler in Braille and asked me to tell Maud about it mentioning that she had used it for her job some years ago. It all seemed unlikely to me but I have found the unlikely things are often very sound evidence. Although she is blind, Maud knows every inch of her small home and she stood up, went to a sideboard and from the very back of one of the drawers produced a folding ruler in Braille. She told me she had used it many years ago, long before I knew her, when she had a job making socks and used the ruler to measure the length. The ruler had been in that drawer for a very long time and I had never seen it nor did I know of its existence. This to Maud, was better than all the telephone calls from people saying that they had 'seen' Michael. Such things are not evidence for they can easily be the product of wishful thinking. A little later I had another experience proving the presence of Michael. He showed me a stage in a hall, not a theatre, more like a church hall or concert hall in a working men's club. He was standing on the stage, singing and dressed in 'drag' as a woman, with a blouse and skirt. When he was younger Michael had a touch of the showman in him and he was full of fun. He would often sit down at the piano and play all the old songs and soon have the whole place singing with him. Maud laughed. She has a remarkable memory which in some ways compensates a little for her blindness, and she could tell me where this concert took place and the year. Again, it was long before I knew them.

I often find that people are disparaging about the usefulness of mediumship. I would not question that if they have had a trivial experience. However, it is not always like that. A friend of mine who is a very good and sincere medium was speaking to an audience a little time back when she felt she must speak to a man near the front of the gathering. She told him that he had a blue car. No doubt he felt he didn't need her to tell him that. She asked him to take it into the garage next morning because there was something wrong with the steering on one side. He questioned it and said that it was unlikely as it was a new car and only a week or two old. She pressed him to do so and he promised her to do it without much enthusiasm. He did so and later rang her to say that the mechanics had found a serious fault and as a result the makers were withdrawing hundreds of similar models for adjustment. I am aware that it would be fine if such a thing was applicable to many aspects of daily life and that Pauline could produce such warnings about all kinds of mistakes. I know she cannot do that day after day, but it doesn't detract from the evidence of what she did on that occasion, nor from the fact that someone was there telling her about the matter. Why this can not be turned on like a tap, especially when it is beneficial – I do not know.

CONCLUSION

Obviously I have not set out to construct a scientific thesis. I have simply shared with the reader some of my experiences and the conclusion to which I have been led; experiences which have reinforced my belief in the Christian Faith. To me these experiences show God's love and goodness by which he gives us further opportunity in the continuation of life, after life in this world to co-operate with His Divine Laws and His will for each one of us. Nothing I have experienced has altered my belief for a moment that we need to turn to Jesus Christ here and now and accept with gratitude what we mean by that old phrase 'His salvation'.

I am not contending with people who crusade against anything allied to the word 'psychic'. However, if there is continuation of life for us all, and if we can only progress in that life not only here but in the following stage of our life to what God has prepared further on, through turning to His Love shown in Jesus Christ, we must surely stop now and think intelligently about our whole position and response. My experiences have proved to me that nobody is outside God's love and His plan for each human soul. I conclude that there is a wonderful and exciting life ahead for those who respond to His invitation of Eternal Life through His Love shown in Christ Jesus and my experiences have proved to me that that life is there even though the pathway of progress may be somewhat different to what I once thought.

12

Neither Shall There be Any More Pain

I promised earlier that I would write briefly about spiritual healing because most mediumistic persons are also very concerned with this ministry. In the last few decades there has also been a renewed interest in spiritual healing in nearly all the Christian Churches.

Pain is part of the world in which we live. Some would argue that it is foolish to put a label on the material world calling it 'imperfect' or 'flawed'. It is simply as it has evolved. Others seek to explain the problems posed by the world of matter in which we live, in terms of man's fall from grace long ago. We can understand the problems that man creates for other people. We have a problem to explain how God, who is Love and Goodness, caused a world to evolve in which there is so much which hurts the human race; all those things for which man is clearly not responsible. Man can upset the balance of nature, he can destroy the ozone layer round the earth, he can pollute the world in which he lives and cause illness through selfish and ignorant use of chemicals on the land. He can, in madness, trigger off cosmic disaster by the wrong use of nuclear power. He is however not responsible for earthquakes and volcanic eruptions, nor for disease and infection which was on the earth long before man himself evolved as we know him. Examination of the remains of creatures which lived long before mankind shows that they were subject to disease.

There is no evidence that the world was once a perfect place with perfect conditions in which the human race could live. Again, some have tried hard to discredit the theories of Charles Darwin about the evolution of the world over millions of years, in

111

order to accept a simple, Genesis-based theory. They claim that Darwin was wrong in his basic assumptions. I have no doubt in the progression of knowledge that some adjustment must be made today in the matter of some details of what he wrote. However, talking to modern scientists I find that basically his view still stands. The world is not perfect and never has been.

I personally take the view that this material world is not meant to be perfect in the sense that nothing should be in it to frustrate, sadden and hurt mankind. To me it is a testing ground; I might almost say a kind of assault course. As man conquers his problems here, so he progresses in character, mentally, psychologically, and spiritually. If conditions were perfect he could not do that. Now I am not saying that God plots out a large number of natural disasters, but seemingly adverse conditions challenge mankind to overcome them and evolve. I believe that evolution or progress continues beyond this world into the vast dimension of the world beyond. The progress is slow by the standards of earth time but I personally feel humbled by the magnitude of the plan. The so-called imperfection of this world has a part to play in that plan. Our eyes, like the eyes of Jesus, must be on the eventual outcome of it all, having absolute confidence in the Love, Goodness and Power of God.

I do not want to be drawn into long theological debate. This is a book for ordinary people. I am not unaware of other points of view, but my contention remains, that the world is a testing ground for our progress. We may not always like it, but there it is!

We want to discuss spiritual healing. There can be little doubt that Jesus was concerned about the suffering of people. We are told that he looked at people with compassion. Sometimes it seems that he was very anxious to get people to listen to the truth of what he was saying and did not want to be famous for being a miracle worker or great healer so that people flocked to him because of that one aspect of his ministry. It is just as evident that he cared about helping people not only to adjust their lives but also felt compelled to heal their minds and bodies. All the four gospels attest the importance of his healing ministry. He expressly commanded his disciples to carry this on in his name. That they did so is also clear from those books of the New Testament which tell us about their activity after they had parted with their master. My last church is dedicated first of course to God and then to St Peter. In the Book of Acts there is a graphic account of Peter healing a lame man who used to sit begging at the gate of the Temple. The man asked for money. Peter said, 'I have no gold or silver but what we have I give you – get up and walk.' He took him by the hand and raised him to his feet and he walked; he not only walked but he leaped and praised God to the astonishment of all that knew him and had seen him sit there begging for years. It is one thing to walk a few halting steps, it is quite another to walk and leap after so many years. People who have been in hospital will tell you that after a long time of inactivity they find normal movement very difficult. That is why today every hospital carries its quota of physiotherapists.

I can remember as a boy going to the swimming baths in Garston. Why I went I cannot now remember – I must have been curious. A revivalist was holding a healing service. I remember an old lady sitting in a wheelchair. The relative who had brought her, replying to the questions of the evangelist healer, told us that the old lady had not stood on her own or walked for many years. The meeting was asked to pray and the healer put his hands on her and she stood up. After a minute or two she walked, at first a few halting steps and then much quicker. The tears streamed down her face and her joy was evident to everyone. I was perplexed. Being a child of my age, I believed in the skill of medical people and medical science. How had this happened? Like many people I knew about the healing of Jesus. Again, like many people I suppose, I tended to think that that was all long ago. I did not look for such things in the modern world. Indeed, at a stage which came a little later I heard people (who for some reason were opposed to non-medical healing) suggest that it was not according to God's plan. Had He not in fact led man to medical advancement? Medical science was a replacement, went the argument, for any past unusual healings. Then critics would declare that in fact many of the so-called healings (they enjoyed that description – 'so-called'!) were not really healings but conditions triggered off psychologically. Some dynamic psychological or nervous event caused the body to refunction. Rather like putting two severed

113

wires together again. Always there were stories which didn't seem to fit in with these objections. For instance I read with great interest of the woman who had been stricken with a very terrible disease which had robbed her of the use of her legs. Her parents had to pick her up and carry her from room to room, caring for her without all the modern aids available today. Her friends prayed for her and all she seemed to do was get worse. Then one day after some years she was sitting alone in a room. She had had no healing from a spiritual healer. Suddenly she felt a warmth come over her and she got up and walked into the next room much to the astonishment, and of course joy, of her people. How had this happened?

When I met Nella Taylor I remember telling her that my mother wished that I had been a doctor. She replied that my mother was a very discerning person. Mrs Taylor had incidentally once given me excellent proof of the presence of my mother. One day Nella had a very bad headache and an important engagement coming along. She said to me, 'Put your hands on my head please.' I did so, and strangely, it did not seem to be an unusual thing to do. I felt a tingling in the palms of my hands and after a short time her headache vanished. She asked me if I ever saw waves of colour and I said that I did and described the colours that I saw. She then told me that I could be used as an instrument of healing and that I ought to pursue this as it was one of the gifts of the Holy Spirit about which St Paul wrote. She did not believe, nor do I that every clergyman has the gift of healing. This ability to be an instrument of healing cuts right across all barriers. It has nothing to do with scholarship or learning, with youth or age, with being a man or a woman.

I then began to take an interest in spiritual healing. I knew about one or two healers in the Church of England. I knew about Dorothy Kerrin at Burrswood and I knew about the pilgrimages to Lourdes. I found that the Spiritualist Church accepted healing as part of the natural function of any church, acknowledging the great Power and Being we call God. As I was investigating psychic matters I had a good chance to talk to healers who went to the Spiritualist Church. I found also that they were frowned upon often by authorities in the orthodox church. Because these authorities did not like spiritualism they dismissed their healing as coming from 'low forces'. It rather smacked of the Jews telling Jesus that he cast out demons by Beelzebub, the Prince of the Demons. Our Lord dealt pretty firmly with that one and told them that he cast out those conditions by 'the finger of God'. I found that some of those who did healing or offered themselves as channels of spiritual healing, did so in the Spiritualist Church because they felt they must give themselves to this ministry under God, and could not do so in their own orthodox churches.

I then met Gordon Turner. Now Gordon was a very highly intelligent man who could have made a fortune in journalism but had instead put his ability to be used as a healing channel at the disposal of God. He still wrote from time to time but demands on his healing were enormous. He once told me that 50 per cent of his 'patients' were sent to him by doctors. That would only happen of course, if those doctors were satisfied that positive results followed his healing – no doctor sends a patient to anyone who is proved to be a failure or a fraud. At heart Gordon was an Anglican, a member of the Church of England although his work was so recognised by spiritualists that he had become President of the National Federation of Spiritual Healers. He lectured at Cambridge and Oxford and spoke at the London Society of Medicine and at many huge meetings in the Royal Albert Hall, the Festival Hall and in Southwark Cathedral. The Bishop of Southwark Mervyn Stockwood incidentally had a great understanding of the things I am writing about in this book. Gordon was quite an expert on meditation. He was a most likeable man, a very humble man and although not blessed with permanent blooming health himself exuded a kind of strong power. He married a delightful lady, Daphne Boden, the famous harpist – Yes, in a Church of England church.

At first I started healing very tentatively but I had a great advantage which Gordon had pointed out. As a vicar going around to people who were sick they would not object, in fact many would more than welcome the laying on of hands. I came to learn that the 'laying on of hands' meant more than at first it seemed. Of course for centuries ordained men had placed their hands on people with prayer, sometimes when they were sick, sometimes to commission them, sometimes out of paternalism. I watched Gordon at work healing and saw that he did what I felt compelled to do without anyone having instructed me. I decided to ask him to help me to launch a healing ministry at St Peter's.

Before I begin to describe some of the aspects of the healing ministry in which I have been active, I wish to comment briefly on spiritual healing generally.

First I find sometimes a conflict about the title of this ministry. Some call it spiritual healing, some call it divine healing and some faith healing. Sadly the conflict is promoted by those who claim that what goes under one heading is inferior to what goes on under another. Christian ministers have not been slow to criticise and 'pooh pooh' the healing ministry of Spiritualists who offer what they term spiritual healing. The critics have attempted to put the ministry of spiritual healers on a lower plane than their own and have preferred to call their own ministry 'divine healing'. The truth is that there is no healing in the fullest sense, no healing to the whole person, body, mind and spirit, except that which stems from God. A healer who acknowledges God and offers his gift to be a channel of healing in the name of God from whom the power comes, is no less a healer for not using the words 'divine healing'. Those who enjoy attacking healers who do not conform to their own ideas of what a healer should say and do ought to remember that, 'God is no respecter of persons.' He will not be confined by the theories of even those who acknowledge and follow Him. We cannot control God or tell Him what He ought to be doing. We cannot insist upon some kind of privileged position because we have some insight into theological truth and give our activity a title which we feel is more acceptable because we would close out those who disturb us by their non conformity. At the same time I believe that it is right to hold fast to the essential factor in healing, that all healing comes from God. If anyone has other beliefs yet does good by healing those who come for help, it does not follow that they are working in conjunction with low forces. God will work as He wills and do what He will do! For me all healing is through Jesus Christ, who we believe was God among us and still meditates His Love and Power to all mankind.

What is this healing? Some would say that it is often simply

116

psychological. The emotions are so stirred that the sick or distressed person is released in their own mind and there is a subsequent physical reaction which may result in the removal of some physical barrier. I think that sometimes in the ministry of a healer, or in a service of healing, that is quite true. A kind of inner explosion or release takes place and there is also physical release from a distressing affliction. Psychiatrists are aiming at this kind of thing, where they feel it is possible, all the time. I do not feel it a criticism of spiritual healing if this should happen at a healing service. Do we not believe that God is solidly behind all the medical work and mental healing of the medical profession? I do. The psychiatrist may discover the factor in the person's past which gives this release. The healer may lead the person to look to God and so put trust in him that the same release is obtained. The important thing is that the condition is bettered.

People often say that any improvement made by a healer is only temporary. I can remember a television programme quite some time ago which showed healing by a Christian evangelist healer. Many such healers are among those who denigrate the work of other spiritual healers. Those 'healed' on the programme seemed certainly to have made an instant improvement. However, a follow-up programme, mentioned that all had over a period regressed. It always amuses me to find that critics of spiritual healing shout in triumph if they find that a person has appeared to be better and then after a period relapses. They do not seem to find the time or energy to constantly attack the medical profession over the thousands of cases where people have ordinary medical treatment and then regress. The medical profession (for which I have a very high regard) is effecting cures by medicine and surgery all the time. Thank God for that. At the same time it is staving off advancing illness very often, holding it back without being able to cure completely and enabling people to cope with their sickness which is most important. I would find it disturbing if there was a great gap between what the medical profession is doing and what spiritual healers are doing. Sometimes we are delighted because a complete cure takes place and, because we are human, often these cures are given great publicity. We would all love to see situations such as those described in the New

117

Testament where Jesus effected a cure which was instantaneous and dramatic. Sometimes this happens. It does not happen every time. Perhaps it is truer to say it does not happen most times. Something is begun but it has to be carried on. Gordon Turner always said to people, 'I want you to go to this or that person who lives in your part of the world and continue the spiritual healing begun today. Often there appeared to be no need for it but he knew there was. Remember that Jesus once went to a certain village and the writer recording what happened wrote, 'He could not do there any mighty work because of their unbelief.' He didn't always have instant success! Doctors tell their patients to take the whole course of treatment, often the patient feels better, abandons the treatment and then relapses. Spiritual healing is often no different. It is a great uplift for the healer when a complete cure seems to have taken place. Often he or she must be content to minister over a long period and simply to give the strength and help necessary to the person so that they can cope with the problem.

There is an interesting account in the Gospels of an event which may very well combine both the Divine Power of Jesus with the kind of skill and insight which today is employed by the psychiatrist. A certain man became mentally ill and violent. The villagers chained him to avoid this violence and caused him to live outside the village. In those days so-called madness was regarded with awe and people were not too keen on dealing stringently with the afflicted person in case the violent spirit which they thought inhabited the person, left him, and entered their own body. They would feed the man but treat him as an outcast. Jesus came upon him on one of his walk-abouts. The account says that a conversation took place between the man and Jesus who went close to him. No doubt the disciples, knowing the man's reputation, preferred to stand off. As they remembered it, so they told the person who set down the account. Jesus talked to the man. Straining their ears the conversation seemed to be about the name of the spirit which had entered the man and made him mad. Apparently under the control of the spirit, he said that his name was 'Legion'. Now in the East possession of 'the name' is important. You do not tell an enemy your name. It gives him power. Jesus so the account says then commanded the spirit to leave the man. During all this a

118

group of pigs, which were nearby feeding, ran off and came to disaster. The disciples, being children of their time, felt that spirits had to have somewhere to go. They could not vanish into thin air and so they deduced that Jesus had 'allowed' them to enter the pigs. This had made the pigs react in the way they had done and come to grief. As a number of pigs came to grief there must have been a number of spirits. There is however a quite reasonable explanation of this graphic event: In subduing Palestine the Roman legions were often very cruel. They were quite ruthless in exterminating opposition. It is quite possible that this man had seen some terrible atrocities during such an attack and the butchering of men, women and children had, as we say, 'turned his mind'. Jesus, like a psychiatrist had probed for the cause of this mental disturbance with great skill, and had ascertained that it stemmed from his experience when the 'Legion' ran amok in his village. Remember, he told him that his (or their) name was 'Legion'. Jesus persuaded the man that he had the power to 'cast out' this terrible experience. He caused him to face it and set it aside by God's Power and Grace. The man was healed from this nightmare which had dominated him for so long. What about the pigs? Did certain evil spirits enter them and cause them to run over a precipice? Personally I don't think so. I think the pigs were so frightened by the shouting of the man and the clanking of the chains (which is described in the account) that they just ran off headlong. People have sometimes sarcastically remarked that Jesus destroyed some pig farmer's livelihood by sending the spirits into the pigs. I don't think so. They ran off and ended up in tragedy.

A spiritual healer will employ his God-given reason, his experience of human nature, his knowledge of life and every aspect of intelligence to help people as well as pray for God's Power and Grace also to operate, very often where all human effort fails.

EPILOGUE

In the tenth chapter of St Luke's Gospel we have the account of Jesus sending out seventy of his followers and commissioning them for their mission. Among the instructions that he gave them was the injunction to 'heal the sick'. In the Book of Common Prayer, deacons are to notify to the priest those who are sick and priests are bidden to minister to them and exhort them, although I suspect that when one is terribly ill the last thing one wants is to be exhorted by anyone. Bishops are told categorically to 'heal' the sick.

It is quite clear that the followers of Jesus obeyed this instruction. They had seen Him heal all types of illness which were beyond the medicine of that day. We tend to refer to these things as miracles. To me the word miracle in connection with Our Lord's ministry does not mean something which is impossible but something quite possible for Him but which is outside our usual experience. If Jesus was, as St John claims, the Lord of All Life, I cannot see why His healing ministry presents a problem. If those of us who seek to be channels of healing do not get His results as often as we would like, that is small wonder. A life of such goodness and purity has not been matched in history, however history may point to many good people who themselves would not want to be mentioned in the same bracket as Our Lord. Such a channel of Divine Power obviously raised no blockage to the flow of healing Grace. The followers of Jesus healed in His name. Peter, in the account I have quoted above described Jesus as the 'Holy One' and the source of healing power. He then went on to elaborate on the person and mission of Jesus and told people about His Resurrection. Many who listened were convinced, and when the next day Peter was hauled before the great council, the Sanhedrin, he was told to cease speaking in that way. He is reported to have said that if it came to deciding whom to obey, man or God, he

120

would obey God. The chief priests threatened him but were fearful that if they took violent action against him and his companions there might be a riot, so warning them, they let them go.

I must say here, because what I will write a little further on may not please some critical persons, that I have never attempted to ask for healing for any person except in the name of Jesus Christ. Every healing meeting I have conducted is in the name of Jesus and I hope this is quite clear.

Man has been concerned with disease from as far back as traditions and records go. His views as to the origin of disease have varied. It has been held in many cultures that disease is the result of the activity of evil spirits. Such views would have said that this applied not only to psychological diseases or disorders as we know them but to every form of illness. To effect a healing the spirit had to be placated or overcome and despatched. Pythagoras declared that disease was caused by demons. Ancient Hindu writings deal with the prevention and cure of disease and whilst surgery and general treatment is mentioned, so also is the use of charms and invocations. In ancient Egypt whilst much was done by way of herbal cures, and by hypnosis, charms and talismans were common. Finnish magicians underwent rites which sought to banish the demons of disease to the furthest frozen parts of their land. No doubt a fitting punishment. Throughout the whole study of ancient people there is a constant theme of striving to master disease and illness and much of course would today be classed as superstition. Sufficient to say that religion and healing were often seen hand in hand and healing was often sought from a power outside the human person whoever or whatever name was invoked in the process. Illness was associated with the assault of demonic forces outside human existence on the mental, spiritual and physical components of man's being. The importance of knowledge was therefore paramount. The priest/healer was able to combat the evil by using the right approach, by enlisting a counter power and very often by getting the unwell person to co-operate by their own free will, placing their faith in the superior power which was to help them.

Modern medicine has been reluctant to acknowledge that spiritual healing is worthy of its blessing. This is understandable in many respects. Scientists on the whole do not believe in demons except those of their own making. Psychologists have little regard for evil spirits but recognise fear and guilt and compulsion as very real adversaries. However the tide is turning. Setting aside all the nonsense, the extravagant and unproven claims and the completely unscientific jargon of some so-called healers which seeks to make medical science unnecessary and misguided and does the cause of spiritual healing no good at all, it is today quite commonplace for doctors to acknowledge that things are achieved by other means than the completely orthodox medical route. The patients that were sent by doctors to that very great spiritual healer and friend of mine, Gordon Turner, did not necessarily stop receiving treatment from those doctors. They were sent to Gordon Turner for the help he could give in tandem with the help offered by the normal medical processes. Orthodox medicine and spiritual healing should go hand in hand. I have known a person say to me that they have told their doctor that they have been having spiritual healing from Canon Quine and the answer has been, 'Good – keep it up.'

We no longer believe all disease and illness is an affliction by evil spirits and demons even if we accept evil possession. I rather tend to think of disease of any kind or disorder of any kind as the negative; the opposite of all that is positive and good invading the mind or the health of the person. It has to be balanced out by the skill of medicine, by faith, by prayer, and by the healing activity of the Living God through Jesus Christ and those who are His servants.

As I have mentioned I often find people trying to differentiate between spiritual healing, divine healing and faith healing. I make no such distinction myself. Faith healing I know, tends to call upon it the sub-title of 'auto suggestion' and the viewpoint that people heal themselves by the operation of their own free will and the victory of mind over matter. I am always glad to see healing and if a person is inspired to gain control of their problem, whatever it is, by the strengthening of their own mind, then I am delighted and not inclined to argue about whether it is a true healing from without or simply the assertion of a correct balance within. In any case I find that even when people draw upon their

122

resources and assert their own mental and spiritual strength, they very often acknowledge the help of a power outside themselves even if they cannot fully break down all its attributes. They just know something happened to them and will not accept that it all happened within themselves.

The phrase 'divine healing' is often jealously claimed by clergy. They like the word 'divine' and many of them are quick to discard all healing which does not come under a certain pattern. For instance they would dismiss all the healing work of Harry Edwards because he was a spiritualist and did not claim that he healed in the name of Jesus Christ. I am disturbed very often by the arrogant way people who do healing within the Christian Church dismiss the work of those who do not belong to it. They fall prey to the age-old sin of exclusivism.

One of the problems before the Church when it began to expand probably under the influence of the mother of the Emperor Constantine and in subsequent centuries, was that it met with pockets of resistance from cultic shrines throughout the world as it followed in the wake of the emperor's legions. The reason for this was that the local people had been in the habit of attending the shrine and/or its priest or holy man, not only to invoke the god of the shrine in a general sense but also to obtain healing. The holy man or priest would not only dispense herbs and remedies, give out armulets and charms and advice often containing precognition, but also effect healing in what we would call a strictly non-medical way. These holy men continued for generations, no matter what opposition they encountered. It is a testimony to the effectiveness of what they did that they survived for so long. I know healers in the church who dismiss all the work of healers of non-Christian bodies as wrong and undesirable. My own view is rather like that of Gamaliel the great Jewish teacher of Paul's time. He felt that the wise thing was to let things stand or fall by their success rate. If it was God-inspired it would prosper, if not it would fall. My view is that there is only one healing – God's healing – and you can call it what you like. That will not alter what He is doing. We do not control God and He is no respecter of persons. If He will work through this person or that, then who are we to say He must not because we have been led along a pathway different from them. That is not to say that our pathway alone is right, nor is it to say that their healing is without His blessing. Whenever people do not like the healer they infer that his healing is temporary and designed to mislead. Did not the opponents of Jesus try it on Him? We have already noted that they said that He was in touch with evil powers. He soon put paid to that argument. The Evil One's whole work is to destroy and disrupt. God desires man's wholeness. The Evil One seeks to overturn God's will. If the Evil One heals and makes whole he is working against himself, as Jesus explained. His hearers were confounded by His logic. All healing flows from God. The way for me is through Jesus Christ but I will not set aside those instances of God working where it is clear He is doing so although there is something unorthodox about it all. My anchorage point is that healing done in the name of the Living God of all Life who is Creator and Sustainer of everything that exists for good in this world, this universe, all universes, and all the spheres of spirit which are vast beyond my imagination and for all I know a good deal more beside all that. In my experience I have not known anyone obtain healing of a permanent character beyond that offered through medicine except by humble acceptance of that great power we call God.

I am often asked if all healers see colour. I have never known one who did not, although there may well be some. Mrs Taylor told me a long time ago about the colours I see. She didn't ask me, she knew I saw such colours. I can always see colours in waves and varying areas whenever I close my eyes and often without closing my eyes. Fear not, it never distracts me when I am concentrating on something which needs my whole attention. I can remember surprising a senior school teacher, in a classroom, when I was talking to senior students about psychic things. I had been requested to do so because she had found that they often dabbled and got into difficulties and she looked to me to set the record right, admit the truth but warn them against such experimentation. In passing I mentioned 'seeing colour' and the teacher asked what I meant. I explained and said that in the room there were bound to be one or two students who saw colour. The look on her face clearly showed that she thought that I was pulling her leg. Having given them confidence by telling them that I saw colour at all times, I asked those who did to put up their hands and to her great amazement several did so. I asked them what colours they saw and explained the significance of them. I just mention this to show that outside us there are forces which we can tap in the quest for spiritual, mental and physical health.

I tend to feel a tingling in the palms of my hands when I am doing healing and those I am trying to help feel excessive warmth from my hands and or a slight vibration. This is generally true with all healers. It is of course one thing to pray with people and I have always been able to do this since my ordination, without embarrassment. People expect it, but to say, 'Would you like me to place my hands on you?' originally was another matter. Now, however I find no awkwardness at all. It seems the most natural thing to do. Ideally, my conception of the way a healing service should work is to have the whole congregation of your church present and praying with you as people come forward for healing. Gordon Turner conducted many healing services but he told me that he much preferred to see people at half-hourly intervals like a doctor, talk with them and then to put his hands on them. This may be well enough for a full-time healer but it is difficult for a man who has many other aspects of daily work.

I have been very fortunate to have the assistance of a first-class healer who is a layman. Unfortunately he has just moved his home to the east coast and we all miss him tremendously. The number of people coming along for spiritual healing has varied down the years from nearly forty to a mere handful. Even if only two or three come along I always feel it is worthwhile. I think like Gordon Turner, it would be better to see people by appointment rather than deal with them all in one service.

I am noted for my sense of humour, and humour does enter into every aspect of dealing with people. I can remember once putting my hands on a man who complained of a swelling at the back, somewhere around his waist. I was a little mystified by the size of the swelling and its location until I found I had my hands on his wallet which he carried under his waist band. Gordon Turner in his book *A Time to Heal* describes how we went to a meeting where the so-called medium insisted on linking him to a man from the other side of life who she said was his father. Now his father was still in this world. She was a very dominant and strange lady and he decided not to take issue with her and to listen with amusement. In a subsequent meeting she elaborated on this 'parent' until says Gordon, 'I became quite fond of him.' She also brought him friends and relatives from the other side of life who also were not dead. Mr Turner and I found common ground in our sense of humour and in the need to balance out the rubbish and nonsense against the truth. It is very easy to dismiss the whole as nonsense because of a bad or silly experience. Gordon both in his mediumship which was greatly restrained and in his healing which was internationally acclaimed was lucid and logical. There were no histrionics with him. No room for humbug. He was a very kindly man and yet a man who could be very firm. People sensed that they were in the presence of great integrity.

I must not conclude this short excursion into spiritual healing without saying something of our experiences at St Peter's. As I have mentioned we began really with that great service many years ago which was conducted by Gordon Turner. He brought with him Daphne Boden, the famous concert harpist, later to be his wife. She was the daughter of an equally famous father who was one of the portrait painters to the Queen. She played the harp beautifully during the service and I was impressed at the way that instrument can be used to convey atmosphere in a church. It was an occasion I will never forget and I am indebted to my church-wardens for backing up the venture which was an entirely new departure for us. Gordon spoke to the packed church and then asked anyone who felt they needed healing to come forward. A number did, and were obviously better for the help. Naturally when recounting experiences of a mediumistic nature as I have done in the other chapters of this book, those which are the most colourful stand out. It is of course true of healing too. The case which comes to mind immediately from that service with Gordon Turner was that of a woman who sat in a side aisle and called to him that she could not come to the front easily because of her complaint. Gordon then went to her and asked me to accompany him. She had a very pronounced curvature of the spine and complications. He instructed me to place my hand on the grotesque displacement and then put his hands on mine. I can only describe the experience by saying that I could feel 'the power' there, whatever that power was. In those days I was learning remember! After a moment he said, 'Take your hand away please,' and he ran his hand down her spine and then said to me, 'Now feel it'. I was astonished, despite the fact that I knew what we were hoping for and seeking to do. Her spine was not absolutely straight but the improvement was dramatic. There was no message. There was no manipulation. She stood up and walked by herself after having been helped into the church by her friends and was overcome with thankfulness. He was quick to ask her to thank God not him. Mr Turner never whipped up people's emotions nor have I ever done. He didn't force people into a kind of psychologically prodded physical effort, which fell apart when people reached home or after a day or so on their own. He always added, 'Now please keep coming along to the church and receive the continual help you need.' I too, though I hope for relief quickly and permanently, would rather see spiritual healing move people forward step by step, giving them the strength to cope with the problems, than to see some quick reaction which is at the heart emotional and which does not last.

Harry Edwards used to take issue with doctors because they seemed to try to find other reasons for his success as a channel of healing. Of course we must see the doctors' point of view. What we need is to take a patient with a complaint which is generally known not to right itself, to document that illness very carefully with the case history, to attach X-rays if necessary and to record all the treatment given. When it is quite clear that medically there is no improvement, to stop medical treatment and to record very carefully with witnesses the nature and times of spiritual healing. If the patient recovers without the aid of any medical help, there needs to be a new set of X-rays and so on until the doctors are convinced that he or she is completely recovered. Unless a scientific approach to spiritual healing is taken in this way, we are not going to get a real hearing from the medical profession in this country which is by nature very conservative. That is not to say that some doctors do not believe in spiritual healing, they do. It will not do to tell the others that we know people who have been cured through the agency of spiritual healing and not by medicine or surgery. On the whole the kind of documentary logging of the illness and treatment I have outlined above does not take place. Indeed often it is not possible. Sometimes people would not submit to it. We tend to let people come along and if they find that they are better or vastly improved, share their satisfaction and pleasure without entering it all in a facsimile of a hospital record chart. Perhaps we are lax in this. In some hospitals in South America there are spiritual healers on the staff but I doubt if their ministry is documented separately from the total medical help offered. Maybe it should not be! St Peter's has been open house in the healing sense for people of all faiths and no religion at all. I have had Hindus come for help and be very grateful for the help received. We have had people belonging to all the Christian Churches.

What kind of thing have we seen happen apart from those things which took place when Gordon Turner came to us? My great friend and Honorary Curate George Jeffs who had a stroke certainly had great help from the healing. Through healing and prayer, and the help of his doctors he was able to continue to officiate at the church and have a good quality of life. I remember a boy who had chronic asthma. You could hear him wheezing when he came into the church at the door. It took about eighteen months but he made a very great improvement. I remember a woman who had a nasty disc displacement condition. She was so delighted with the help from the spiritual healing that she not only wrote thanking us but made a generous donation to the work. I recall a very dear soul who had cancer and was given two months to live by her consultant who gently told her she should put her affairs in order. She came regularly to the healing service and the months passed into a year and one year into the next. Her consultant said to her, 'I have been honest with you, tell me what are you doing?' She said, 'I am going along to Canon Quine's healing service at St Peter's.' He just said, 'Fair enough, I knew that you were doing something!' She passed onwards in due course after this extension to her life in which she was able to go to Australia to see her family. She was so grateful for that extension and all she had been able to do in that time. She was almost blind too and she had a lovely golden retriever as a guide dog who accompanied her to church and lay at her feet during the healing service. He used to go to sleep and snore, much to our amusement – I love animals and I miss him.

I have written elsewhere about the little girl who had leukaemia. She too had an extension of life beyond the forecast of her doctors through the spiritual healing. During this time her parents were able to come to terms with the situation and to absorb the truth that although the body was so distressed that the healing was having only a partial effect, nevertheless as with all who receive spiritual healing, the inner self and the mind were also receiving healing. We all need that, even those of us who think we are well! They came to understand that their little girl would put aside the physical body but in every way a complete person would continue in the life God had prepared for her ahead.

I recall a good friend of mine who has been a top-class bowler. I will never forget him for many reasons, not least because when we had a very nasty fire in the vicarage due to an electrical fault, and were in absolute chaos, he just looked around and didn't waste words. He said, 'If you want any money let me know.' I didn't avail myself of that kind offer but I did appreciate it. He suddenly found that he needed to have an ulcer removed from his stomach. He went into hospital in June and the surgeon operated on him. I met the surgeon one day and said 'What have you done to my friend Mr Branston? 'Why,' he said, 'I have removed two thirds of his stomach.' This friend had spiritual healing a number of times and in late August he won his Bowling Club Pairs Competition. I am quite sure the spiritual healing played its part.

We have had a number of people who have benefitted from this ministry after heart problems, others who have had ease with painful joints or who have suffered from stress. One of the funniest things I can recall was a very good soul in my congregation who developed disc trouble and her doctor put her on a board on the floor to sleep. She was in great discomfort. I visited her one day and gave her spiritual healing by placing my hands upon her back and she was very much better in a few hours and gradually the condition improved. Her doctor was a little

129

suspicious at the speed of the recovery and he asked her if she had been to an osteopath or a chiropractor. 'No,' she said, 'I have been to the vicar.' I saw the funny side of that and would have given much to see the doctor's face.

Down the years we have had a steady stream of people with some very serious complaints and some with less serious illnesses, all who have benefited from this ministry in varying degrees. Often the sad thing is that people come along when they have exhausted all other conventional means of help. I have often sighed and felt that it would be nice to get a patient who had the first twinge of arthritis and who in answer to my question, 'How long have you had it friend?' replied, 'Just a few weeks vicar,' instead of 'Ten years.' I would like to see spiritual healing as part of the total help offered to sick people and accepted by doctors and society as a whole. We are still a long way from that I am afraid. Looking back I am sorry in some ways that I never carried out the kind of documentation which would have supported spiritual healing better and afforded concrete evidence. On the other hand I suppose that what matters is that people came along, and were helped on their way through life and were thankful to God. Perhaps in the future some younger person will begin the kind of spiritual healing ministry, carefully documented in a manner acceptable to the medical profession, which will open the way for the kind of co-operation which existed between Gordon Turner and his medical friends. I am aware of course today that there are some medical practices where doctors are now happy to incorporate into their medical centre the services of a spiritual healer if people would like to also have that help. Let us hope that this will increase as the years go by.

I know that the Church now takes very seriously this matter of spiritual healing and that there is a centre where spiritual healers can be trained. I was pleased to see a television documentary which covered this centre and to see that the way potential healers were being trained was very much along the lines into which I have been led. One word of warning however! We must remember St Paul's remarks about the gifts of the spirit. The gift of being a channel of healing power (and no healer is more than that) is not universal. Just as there are those who think they have the mediumistic gift and only have one or two unusual experiences who will never be able to offer a consistent ministry of this kind, so there are those who would like to be healers or who think the gift of being such goes with some other office but who are not really channels of healing power. I know that sometimes prayer alone can see astonishing things happen. Thank God for that. However in healing we need to be very careful not to be sentimental or imaginative and to recognise that much more than good intentions are necessary.

I hope that you have enjoyed reading this small book. Its purpose is to make people think. If it has done so I am glad I have 'stuck by' what I know to have been true situations. I wish that you could have had some of the experiences I have been privileged to undergo. I can however share some of them with you.

KEN QUINE